PUSHCART

Nonfiction
His Son
Her Father
Tower
All My Dogs
Cathedral

Fiction
The Kid That Could

Poetry
The Family Bible

As Editor
The Pushcart Prize Series
The Publish-it-Yourself Handbook
The Art of Literary Publishing
Rotten Reviews
Minutes of the Lead Pencil Club
Love Stories
(Series with Genie Chipps)
The Pushcart Book of Short Stories

Letters to My Grandsons

Bill Henderson

PUSHCART PRESS
WAINSCOTT, NEW YORK

Distributed by W.W. Norton & Co.
ISBN 979-8-985-4697-7-6

NOTE TO THE READER

This collection of letters, memoir excerpts, clippings and journal entries was originally assembled privately for my grandsons. Friends have suggested it might be useful to others. I hope it is of some interest and value to you.

MY OBLIGATION IS TO BE A GOOD ANCESTOR.
Dr. Jonas Salk

Dear Boys,

This is the message I wish my own grandfather had written to teenage me. But he never did.

He had been around—up and down—that grandfather, my Pop's dad. Born just seven years after the Civil War ended, Grandpop Henderson grew up into the age of the automobile, the airplane, motion pictures, the Depression, radio, phonographs, the pandemic of 1918, World Wars I and II, the Atomic Bomb, television, and the Cold War. In short, he was the custodian of a vast expanse of American and personal history. He was a salesman and delivery guy for Swift and Company, meat packers. He had been drunk and sober, married (not well) to a born-again wife, and he had fathered three sons. He knew a lot and was in his old age (my age as I write this letter) totally silent.

He said nothing to teenage me. No advice, no praise, not more than a glimmer of words about his 80 plus years. Like his son, perhaps grandpop thought men should remain stoic and quiet. Complaining or gushing in happiness was unmanly. Or maybe he was just very old and very tired of it all.

All my other grandparents were long dead. He was all I had.

As I am now his age (and you are very young), I remember as a kid how I'd wished he would talk to me, tell me what to expect as I grew up, some advice, some humor, a letter or two from the old age home where he spent his final year, sitting motionless in a chair.

I may soon end up like him, so I write to you twins William and Hunter with some urgency. Right now I am in good health. Brain crackles, muscles still muscle. Your grandmother Genie and I are employed in jobs we value. We imagine that we are still useful to our neighbors and society, contributing a bit of love and help when needed. But in our 80s all of that may vanish in a moment—strokes, accidents, cancers—the whole list of elderly cancelations may hit either one of us.

In fact, there is a good chance that you won't read this until you are young adults and I am long gone. Right now you are five years old, a wonderful, happy pair. Your smiles make living a joy for us weary adults. Your love for your parents, Lily and Ed, embraces the entire universe. I feel at times that your innocence is exactly what Jesus meant when he said ". . . unless you become as children you will not enter the kingdom of heaven."

So in a way, Hunter and William, you are my teachers. You inspire me to write this.

My hope is that these letters may return some of the love and wonder that you are now offering me in my 80 years. Plus a bit of advice to take or leave, as you will.

My temptation has been to write a long tome of suggestions and practicalities based on my checkered history of self, indeed a list of mistakes, lucky breaks and the 50 years of Pushcart Press. But I have already attempted that in six memoirs, over many years, all modestly sold and all still in print. The memoirs concern my rather ordinary life that was somehow touched by guidance and grace from an unknown source. But more on that later.

This is a collection that I thought you might ponder, plus passages adapted from my efforts at memoir. I hope all this might touch and inspire and caution you, a smorgasbord for your pilgrim walk.

You can read day by day or skip around, or plow through the entire book at once.

Of course you can skip the whole thing and set out on your own without the musings of an altekocker (look it up).

So much will confront you in the years ahead. We have left you a morbidly ill planet, ruined by greed, power grabs and shopping madness. We call ourselves "consumers," as if that is an honorific, and we call our mess "climate change."

Even worse is the rising tyranny of technology. Somehow, out of nowhere and for no necessary reason, we have constructed a digital universe that seeks to control and trivialize the human animal. Soon machines will take over and we will be an insignificant blip in the guts of a future computer. All our million-year history forgotten, a carbon-based evolutionary error.

But I will save my preaching for the letters that follow.

Such a huge, maybe impossible task you two face.

But you will have help from so many good and able grandparents, parents, cousins and friends. And you have each other. Twins! Identical! You know each other well and can help better than a grandpappy from far away.

And, the Great Mystery willing, your extraordinary and loving parents will be with you for decades too.

As for me, I may be dust, but I hope that dust means a little more to you in these jottings from the past.

At the very least this book may help me fill in the silence from my own grandpop.

> Love and wonder,
> Grandpappy

P.S. There is no particular order for the letters, quotes, clippings and you may find they often contradict each other. Make up your own mind.

IT COULD BE THAT OUR FAITHLESSNESS IS A
COWERING COWARDICE BORN OF OUR VERY
SMALLNESS, A MASSIVE FAILURE OF IMAGINATION
. . . IF WE WERE TO JUDGE NATURE
BY COMMON SENSE OR LIKELIHOOD, WE
WOULDN'T BELIEVE THE WORLD EXISTED.
Annie Dillard

Dear Boys,

You guys or your children may never know a childhood like my own, infused with God, as an unspeakably horrifying World War raged. So here is a glimpse into that long ago time that I know was just as loving as your own home in a different way.

In those 1940's suburban morning breakfasts, my Mom, your great grandmother, squeezed oranges for fresh juice, dosed us with cod liver oil (she remembered the foul odor of the oil) mixed the Ovaltine and cooked hot cereal. Pop sitting between my sister Ruth in her highchair my brother Bobby and me, spooned his cereal and listened to Reverend Carl McIntire's "Twentieth Century Reformation Hour" on the radio. Reverend McIntire shouted that the Communists were advancing across Europe and the Russians would soon have the A-bomb and that meant the End was near just as predicted in Revelation: "Behold I am coming soon, bringing my recompense, to repay every one for what he has done . . . Blessed are those who wash their robes, that they may have the right to the tree of life and that they may enter the city by the gates. Outside are the dogs and

sorcerers and fornicators and murderers and idola-
ters, and everyone who loves and practices false-
hood."

Reverend McIntire's words—even the few I
understood—didn't scare me, and neither did his
sadistic frenzy. My Pop knew Reverend McIntire's
God and what that God required of us, Pop loved us
and wouldn't lie to us. Pop and God would see that
we were on the right side in the coming terror. The
rule for kids was Be Good. Pop and God would take
care of the rest.

Mother, who liked just about eyerybody—and
was liked in return—treated everybody as if they
were good: the Degger's Dairy delivery milkman,
the Freihoffer's bread man, the teachers, the minister, most of the neighbors. Pop, in his short breakfast grace, murmured under Reverend McIntire's
shrieks, would often include President Harry Truman in his list of good, God-fearing men.

To Pop, sin was real. Sin was the cause of everything terrible. Heaven and hell were actual places.
Jesus and God were people who lived with us. The
events of the world and of our every day were
crammed with meaning and grand purpose.

Pop did not speak directly about such matters. He
let Reverend McIntire do that.

When McIntire, complained—as he often did—
that he was too poor, that the devil was at the door
and he couldn't possibly continue his radio ministry
unless all his listeners rushed him money, I wrote:
"Dear Dr. McIntire, my name is Billy and I am in
bed with measles. I like your program. Here is twenty-
five cents. This is my allowance for the week. I will
send you another twenty-five cents next week."

Reverend McIntire read my letter on the air and
declared that it was most touching to get that kind
of contribution from a bedridden child and wouldn't
God be pleased if everybody sacrificed like that. He
mailed me a purple plastic spoon "to feed the gospel
to the world" and a small red velvet wall plaque that
told me in gold letters "I can do all things through
Christ which strengthenest me. John 3: 20."

"All things!" I wondered. I could do "all things"
as long as I pleased Jesus by cleaning up my room,
memorizing my Sunday School Bible verses, getting
good report cards, and not picking my nose.

With such assurances I began my young life in
suburban Philadelphia.

The opposite of faith is not doubt but certainty.
Anne Lamott

Dear Boys,

I suggest that you always have a good dog in your life.

My first dog Trixie, a rescue mutt, was blessedly wordless. She kept me informed about another universe far from the theological threats and posturing of adults. Her pack did not deal in pathetic attempts at verbal definitions—a bark sufficed. They didn't twist themselves in knots of murderous argument about salvation, gender, race, or political creed. They were content to just be. To chase a black rubber ball and wrestle with me until my hands were red from her happy teeth was *joy* enough for Trixie.

Play was Trixie's God. In the beginning was Play. Her worship demanded only that she diligently chase her ball. She and I worshipped daily from an overstuffed blue couch. I tossed her ball into the corners of our tiny living room and Trixie retrieved it, jumped on the couch, made me grab the ball from her mouth, and set off when I threw it again. As we battled in doggie bliss, I seldom realized the deadly and growing seriousness of my seven-year-old life.

Dear Boys,

When I was a kid, we had radio and then tv and Pop concocted a record maker. The real high tech was still to come.

Mother allowed us one radio program an evening. My favorite was "Sergeant Preston of the Yukon and His Dog, King," a serial about battling wickedness in the frozen north. Bobby and I sat on the living-room rug with our ears a few feet from the speaker. When King was shot by claim jumpers and presumably killed, Bobby and I cried for hours and missed dinner. But King got better for the next evening's episode.

Late in the 1940s Pop bought a gigantic second-hand television that, through a mirror, reflected images of the Lone Ranger, Buster Crabbe, Bob Steele, Tom Mix, and Howdy Doody.

Some evenings, on his homemade record-maker, Pop recorded his children playing their musical instruments. He also recorded our first words, our birthday parties, and Pop's own recitations. "Trust and obey," Pop recited from the hymn of that title, "for there's no other way to be happy in Jesus but to trust and obey."

When the newspapers headlined that momentous speeches were scheduled, Pop readied his record-maker by the radio. Here's Harry Truman announcing the first H-bomb test explosion and the dawn of extinction: "The world will have peace through fear."

As I do, you guys probably still live in that fear of total extinction. It's not a good place to be. Our mad inventors continue to take us near oblivion, through bombs or robots or whatever has been concocted in your day. They invent stuff just because they can but they are often leading us into disaster. Resist the amoral wizzbangs.

Take that rock over there, it doesn't seem to be doing much of anything, at least to our gross perception. But at the microlevel it consists of an unimaginable number of atoms connected by springy chemical bonds, all jiggling around at a rate that even our fastest supercomputer might envy . . . you might think of the rock as a purely contemplative being. And you might draw the moral that the universe is, and always has been, saturated with mind.

Jim Holt

Dear Boys,

In the suburban evenings, we kids—Bobby, Ruth and me—were bathed, dressed in our pyjamas and tucked in to our beds by Mom, who then supervised our evening prayers: "Now I lay me down to sleep, Pray the Lord my soul to keep. If I should die before I wake . . ."

I didn't know what a "layme" was and the thought that I might die made no sense.

Then I recited the Lord's Prayer and my personal requirements such as penance for being bored in church, or opening my eyes while praying, or even thinking "damn," or accidentally ripping a page of a Bible, or bumping a parent—the Bible said that parent-strikers were to be stoned to death without qualifications—or disobeying any of the Ten Commandments, including the ones I didn't understand like "Thou Shalt Have No Other Gods Before Me" (what did "Before" mean?) or "Thou Shalt Not Covet Thy Neighbor's Wife, or His Ass or His Manservant" (what did "Covet" mean and wasn't "Ass" a bad word?) or "Thou Shalt Not Commit Adultery" ("Adultery" was said so hesitantly by my parents that I wasn't about to ask them what it meant; just to pronounce the word out of Biblical context might be a sin).

In every evening prayer I asked God to destroy all the bars in the world and replace each with a church. That was a priority request. Pop assured us that nothing was worse than a bar.

I finished my prayers with "in Jesus' name," because if I left that off, I'd be praying like a Jew. I didn't know much about Jews. Only one Jewish family lived on our block but they were supposed to be different in some strange way.

In the night while the drum-major music-box lamp played "Twinkle, Twinkle Little Star," my brother and I held hands between our beds. This was our insurance against the dreaded man in the attic, or the dark presence in the cellar, or the bogey man lurking just outside our bedroom window in the lilac bush (the same bush that each spring filled our room with the fragrance of its blossoms).

A few steps down the hall Mom and Pop read the Bible to each other and said their own prayers before sleeping.

And in the arms of a loving God we all slept.

Their door was left open a crack so that Mother could hear our calls or cries. Once every night one of us would ask her for a glass of water and Mother, uncomplaining, would wake and bring the water. We were seldom really thirsty. We just wanted to be sure she was still there. Soothed, we would fall asleep again, listening to the distant clack-clack of the trolley to Philadelphia.

Long after her children were grown and no longer needed her to bring water in the night, her door was still left ajar. She still listened.

In my memory of her, I see again your own mother's perpetual caring for you two since the second you were born and even before when she sang to you in her womb: "I'll be a living sanctuary for you . . . holy, bright and true."

If you ever are depressed or discouraged, remember Lily singing to you. Hear her voice, honor her song.

Earth: a mote of dust suspended in a sunbeam.
Carl Sagan

Here's something I know to be true, although it's a little corny and I don't know what to do with it: What I regret most in my life are failures of kindness.

George Saunders

Dear Boys,

I was lucky to have had rather odd elementary school teachers long ago. They did not teach so that we could pass standardized tests, as is the current fad. They taught from the gut, and some had odd guts—with theological implications.

In Penn Wynne elementary school I learned about the Permanent Record. This record was similar to God's heavenly record and to the less important records of Santa Claus and Peter Rabbit.

The Permanent Record was kept by Mrs. Morris, the principal, and would be on file on earth forever. When somebody crayoned "Minnie Morris" on the school wall—meant as an unflattering comparison of our principal to the cartoon Minnie Mouse—we were warned that the insulting child had to confess to Mrs. Morris or the crime would be entered on the Permanent Record of every child.

Nobody confessed.

Our moral supervisor in kindergarten was Mrs. Hotchkiss. She assured the class that if we didn't quiet down, the crack in the ceiling would widen and the entire ceiling would plunge down on us. We could see the crack growing every day, couldn't we, just look up there.

If the crack didn't work, she threatened us with the Stuff, a mysterious substance stored in a brown jar on the top shelf of the closet. Mrs. Hotchkiss said that the Stuff, when smeared on a child's lips, would glue the mouth shut for three days. That meant you couldn't eat, talk, or drink water. The Stuff meant death.

Evil to Mrs. Hotchkiss was Chucky Charles. She knew awful things about Chucky that none of us knew and she was constantly ordering Chucky to sit in the dark immense hall by himself for mysterious crimes.

We were weaving potholders one day, when suddenly a shrieking Chucky was being dragged across the room toward the Stuff. Chucky wet his pants and the class cried with him, "No, no, no, Mrs. Hotchkiss!"

She reached up to the shelf and held the brown bottle in Chucky's face. She looked at us for a while, stared down at the writhing Chucky, and slowly untwisted the top. When we were all screaming loud enough to bring down the ceiling, she smiled and put the Stuff back on the shelf.

Something changed for me that day.

Mrs. Hotchkiss had tortured us. But she was the teacher, the supposed good person. I suspected she was just as evil as she said Chucky was. And I didn't understand that.

In third grade, the class watched tadpoles change into frogs. Most of the tadpoles had four legs and were just beginning to lose their tails, when Barry Lurton—a kid with the habit of grinning and simultaneously touching his tongue to the point of his nose—heaved the aquarium out of the second-floor window.

As we stood around the broken glass and almost-frog bodies, our third-grade teacher Mrs Light tried to console us. "It wasn't Barry's fault," she said.

Wasn't Barry's fault? I wondered. Then whose fault was it?

Sure, Barry was "retarded," but it was still his fault. Otherwise, the deaths must be God's fault because God made Barry the way he was.

But that was unthinkable.

Barry went to special school the next week and I tried to forget about it.

But, of course, you boys will not be able to forget the horrendous unfairness around you and far away. Don't bother to blame God.

Do something to help.

The trouble with Christianity is not that it has been tried and found wanting, but that it has not been tried at all.

G.K. Chesterton

When rejected remember that you are a pilgrim on a sacred journey. Get up and start walking again.

BH/Journal

Dear Boys,

It used to be that Sundays were a quiet day for the entire country. Few businesses were open. God was supposed to be our focus.

I was taken to Philadelphia's Oak Park Presbyterian Church when I was a month old. I graduated from the nursery, and the sandbox, and soon sat in the primary grade wearing my first tie, decorated with a Day-Glo flamingo.

On my sports coat was a Sunday School attendance pin with three bars on it, indicating five years of perfect attendance—a pin for the first year, a wreath around it for the second, and bars underneath for following years. My goal was the world's United Presbyterian Church record of forty-four years perfect attendance. That man's pin was framed on the church wall.

Primary school services began with a teacher's prayer and some hymns: "Jesus wants me for a Sunbeam, a Sunbeam, a Sunbeam / I'll be a Sunbeam for Him." Then we were asked to stand and recite a Bible verse we had been assigned to memorize last Sunday. For this we were graded on a wall chart with gold, silver, and blue stick-on stars.

After years of Sunday School most stories became yesterday's news. Some of the bored kids sailed paper airplanes past the teacher and one boy heaved a hymnal across the room when he was scolded for failing to memorize all the books of the New Testament in order. Just in time we were graduated to intermediary grade. A male teacher kept order.

Here I learned that I had not only sinned from time to time, but that I was a Sinner. "Mr. Mitchell, what do you mean we are all Sinners? I'm not!" I cried out.

"Yes, you are, Billy. Every human is a Sinner."

What was the use of even trying to be good if you ended up in the same category as real sinners? Mr. Mitchell must have made a mistake about me and other good people. For instance, there were people who went to bars and there was me.

For church services after Sunday School the family, led by Mother, walked down the church aisle to the second pew from the front. We sat up there because Mother said the minister would get lonely if everybody sat near the middle and back of the church. Also, Bobby, Ruth, and I tended to behave on display like that.

One Sunday in late summer 1949 a new evangelist came to our summer place in Ocean City, New

Jersey. Billy Graham pitched a huge tent in a gravel parking lot. I sat at the back of the tent on a wooden folding chair next to Pop and was fascinated about what Billy had to say about a Christian man who lapsed from the faith and began drinking and going with women. He stopped tithing and bought a Jaguar sports car with his tithing money. The man knew God was angry with him and he promised God that he would reform and God listened to him and welcomed him back. But the man lapsed again, and begged forgiveness, and was forgiven, and then lapsed again. Finally, God would not listen any more to his pleas. The man begged and begged but God had had it. The man parked his Jaguar on the Ben Franklin Bridge and jumped off.

At the end of the sermon, Billy asked all of us who wanted to be saved to raise our hands. I had thought I was saved from the day I put my hand on top of the radio, like Carl McIntire told us to do, and said "I believe." But you couldn't be too sure about such things. I didn't want to end up like the Jaguar man who stopped tithing.

Billy pointed around the room, counting hands and acknowledging salvations. I leaned forward in my seat and waved my hand so that he wouldn't miss me, and I looked over at Pop. Pop had his hand raised too. He smiled and nodded at me. I had pleased him greatly and I was glad.

Outside on the boardwalk—surrounded by vacationers in shorts sucking on ice-cream cones and frozen custard, pushing baby carriages and trailing balloons, banging at pin-ball machines and blasting rifles at metal ducks—I felt exactly how I had been told I was supposed to feel. I was pounds lighter. My sins had been lifted from me. I was floating. I was certain that the crowd could see me floating.

"Saved!" I wanted to shout as we walked down the boardwalk toward home. And now Pop and I would save the whole world! This was no ordinary Saturday night stroll. This was a march, a march to banish sickness and pain and evil and war from the world and bring in Jesus Christ. Holding Pop's hand, I wanted to put my other arm around everybody on the boardwalk. Pop and I were marching for Jesus and we'd conquer the continents for Him.

The next morning I felt just as light and sin-free. But I was a little worried. Had the evangelist really seen my hand? It was a small hand. I was a small boy. Perhaps he'd missed my hand in the crowd. If he had, was I saved for sure?

Sunday evenings Pop sometimes took me to the Baptist Church. The four sides of its short steeple announced in red neon to the town below "Jesus Saves." I liked the evening services here because they showed the missionary society's movies of unsaved Hindus worshipping cows, and walking through burning coals. Being a Christian was obviously better than that, and I had a mission to change such foolishness.

One winter afternoon I was suddenly inspired. "Pull your sleds around me in a circle," I told the younger kids. They sat on their sleds and dug their galoshes into the snow while I told them that John 3, verse 16, said: "Whosoever believeth in me shall have eternal life," and that if they didn't believe in Jesus they would go to hell, and that it was important to go to church every Sunday. The six Mahoney kids didn't attend church at all, Pop informed me. I was particularly worried about them.

I told the kids we would meet every Sunday on our sleds in my backyard until all of them had accepted Jesus into their hearts. But next Sunday I found I had nothing new to say and we sledded off in search of more interesting play. And we played without ceasing.

To say that God can only truly be revealed in scripture, as many have insisted through the ages, is a little like saying that, even if you live right across the street from the ball park with a lifetime free pass, the best way to follow the Yankees is to read about them in the papers . . .

Rev. Rob McCall

GRACE—

TO BE ACCEPTED BY THAT WHICH IS

GREATER THAN YOU.

Paul Tillich

Imagination is how we know God.
Joan of Arc

Dear Boys,

 This letter is about fathers, mine and yours.

 Your father Ed adores you. Your life may take you far away from Ed, but never forget his love.

 My Pop too adored his kids. How wonderful to have such love in our young lives.

 I remember that when I was sick Pop rushed upstairs after arriving home from work. He knelt by my bed, his hand on my fevered forehead, praying aloud for my recovery. Sometimes I was happy to be missing school. I was embarrassed by his passion. Mom's doctors and prescriptions were fast enough for me.

 When I was well, I played the evenings away outside with the neighborhood kids. Pop called me in for dinner with his two-fingered, two-note whistle, which was unlike the plastic whistles, hoohoos, and bells of other parents. Often he had brought home small gifts from work for each of us, and handed them to us as we kissed his scratchy whiskers.

 I remember a metal globe. My father handed me the world.

 On summer evenings in Ocean City Pop and the family walked the boardwalk in the twilight. We stopped at the Litterer's Fresh Orange Juice Parlor for tall glasses of just-squeezed orange juice and walked back to our summer house.

Near the orange juice place was a tiny shop that sold novelties—Mexican jumping beans, miniature New Testaments, the Lord's Prayer on a penny, and, on this one night, baby soft-shelled turtles. As a nine-year-old turtle collector, I knew that the soft-shell—with protruding eyes, a long snout, and flat leathery shell—was said to be more dangerous than a snapping turtle. I bought one for fifty cents.

For two years the ugly soft-shell grew in my bedroom aquarium while the more colorful dime-store terrapins around him lived a few months on dried fly turtle food and died. The soft-shell ate anything, from tomatoes to dog food, with a hearty viciousness and thrived. I thought he was immortal.

One night I put the soft-shell in the bathroom sink while I soaked his aquarium in suds. I ate my dinner and afterward found that a slow drip from the hot-water tap had scalded the turtle to death.

I carried his body to Pop. Pop rushed the turtle to his basement workshop and attached him to a small generator he had built—the front foot to one wire, the back to another.

I whirled the handle of the generator as he instructed and the turtle twitched. "Faster," Pop ordered.

I cranked furiously and the soft-shell shivered. We both hoped that it was the reviving turtle and not just the jolts of electricity that caused the shivers. I cranked until both arms were sore, and then Pop cranked.

But when we detached the turtle from the generator, he was still.

Pop had done all he knew how.

It was the first time Pop and I met death together. We met it with kindness. That's about all I can suggest. We are all going to die, and all we have is each other in an infinite universe. Crank the generator and keep on cranking.

I THINK I COULD TURN AND LIVE WITH
ANIMALS, THEY'RE SO PLACID AND SELF-
CONTAIN'D. I STAND AND LOOK AT THEM
LONG AND LONG. THEY DO NOT SWEAT
AND WHINE ABOUT THEIR CONDITION,
THEY DO NOT LIE AWAKE IN THE DARK AND
WEEP FOR THEIR SINS, THEY DO NOT MAKE
ME SICK DISCUSSING THEIR DUTY TO GOD.
Walt Whitman

LIAM

At church, my turn to read
The lesson from my beat up Bible,
(Presented to "Billy" Oak Park
Sunday School, Philadelphia, 1949).

I recite that David defeats
The Moabites, executes two out of
Three prisoners face down in dirt
And praises the God we worship.

Afterward I float from the bleeding
Altar, wondering what I am doing
Back here among the bloody Christians
Of my childhood,

A seven year old spirit,
Little suffering Liam the epileptic,
Appears from the pews.
A football helmet on his head,
His protection from daily seizures.

Liam hugs my knees hard.
Wordless.

I toss the Bible in a pew.
Now I know what I am doing
Back here.

Dear Boys,

My brother Bobby and I took care of each other while growing up. Violence in our house was unknown.

However, as we both neared puberty one Christmas, we made a symbolic exception, with boxing gloves.

Early in December, Pop climbed the ladder to the attic and handed down the boxes that stored the Lionel train set—the tracks, the station, the cattle feed pen, the model village, an old-fashioned steam engine, freight cars, the transformer and switching gear, the diesel Santa Fe Flyer engine and passenger cars (a light lit up the inside of the cars and we could see the passengers silhouetted). On the living-room floor, we pieced together a rail line around the edges of the room, under the Christmas tree and sometimes even out to the dining room and back again.

And on that divine birthday morning of all mornings, Bobby, Ruth, and I huddled at first light at the top of the stairs, waiting for Mom and Pop to join us in the rush down to the Christmas tree to discover what Santa had left us, and what marvelous gifts Pop had been secretly making in the basement, off-limits to us for months before. (One year it was a terrific wooden wagon, with rubber-treaded, handcrafted wooden wheels and "Bill & Bob" painted on the side.)

And so, pyjamaed and taking turns, as instructed by Mom, we unloaded our Christmas stockings first and then ripped into the wrapped stuff from relatives, Mom, Pop, and Santa. (We noticed Santa had finished off the milk and cookies we left for him by the fireplace the night before.) Wrapping paper and ribbons flew about the room or were used to decorate our mutts of the moment, Trixie and Duke.

In one shameful Christmas season, when I was approaching my noisome adolescence, Mom and Pop asked what I wanted that year, and I demanded boxing gloves. My pacific father was particularly appalled by the request. Boxing!! I was pulling a manly pose for him. To my sorrow, he went for it. On Christmas Day I fitted on the gloves—Bob (no longer Bobby) also got a pair—and we belted each other a few times. Our manliness proven, the gloves went back in their boxes, never to reappear. Our Christmases remained seasons of peace.

As twins, and sometime rivals, you boys may be tempted from time to time to smack your brother. Resist the urge. He is after all your original best friend.

In 2003, George W. Bush, our born-again Christian President ("Jesus changed my life") declared "shock and awe" on the people of Baghdad. We got to see his sacred war live on TV, thousands of innocents ("collateral damage") slaughtered in massive explosions, like a Fourth of July extravaganza. I and much of the world had protested Bush's oil-mad extermination. It was hopeless. We had no say. The administration faked its way into made-for-TV entertainment with embedded reporters chattering their way through the desert in tank bellies.

By now this unspeakable fraud is old news, but I wondered then, and still do, how is it that we roast people as if at a suburban barbeque? What a waste of good meat. After Jonathan Swift's "A Modest Proposal" I suggest a screed on the economic wisdom of cannibalism. Why waste all this tender flesh? Harvest it from corpses and can it. If

human consumption of humans turns you off,
pack it for pigs.

BH/journal entry

Dear Boys,

In Deer Isle, Maine is a little cemetery lost in the woods. While hiking one day, Lily and Genie and I discovered the tombstones of John Toothacker and his wife Elizabeth who died after the Civil War; surrounding them were the five small stones of their young children, Mary, James, Thomas, Abigail, and Edward, all dead in the same year, 1834, from some nameless disease. Yet on all of the tombstones were messages of faith.

I can't even begin to imagine what vision it took to sustain that mother and father through such a year. There was no talk therapy in 1834, no calming pills; nothing but a faith that all this horror had to mean something, somewhere, somehow. We inherit that faith, and if we neglect it, we dishonor those two parents and millions of people before us.

I invite you boys to consider that faith, ignore its many historical and present faults. Skip the ghastly appropriations of the power hungry. Go to the essence: love and wonder.

Dear Boys,

When I first fell in love it was with the minister's daughter, Lois. She was quiet and shy with pale brown hair that I exaggerated in fantasy to movie-star blonde. At eleven I couldn't think of a thing to talk to her about, and I was too lightheaded whenever within a few feet of her to talk anyway.

One Sunday afternoon we went to the minister's house for dinner. I wandered into Lois's bedroom, found her there, and not knowing what else to do, sat next to her on the bed wordlessly. Pop and the minister looked into the room. "Oh they're . . ." Pop blurted. I bolted up and left the room, realizing I had done something too awful for Pop to mention.

I dreamed of Lois. In the dream we were together on a small bridge over a moonlit pond. I would swoon and fall into the pond.

I carried her photograph in my Roy Rogers wallet, and one night as Pop and I drove home from Sunday night hymn singing, I confessed to him that I was in love with Lois.

Pop said he had fallen in love once too, with Mom, and it was important to love only a good Christian woman.

For a few miles we were men in love together. It was the only time we ever talked about girls, about women.

Advice: If you have just arrived at puberty and happen to fall in love with the minister's innocent daughter—and he is of the anti-sex theology—and if you are alone in the bedroom with his daughter, fall on your knees and pray. Wait long enough for your new erection to subside. Then rise and praise the Lord.

Dear Boys,

On June 9, 2021, when you boys were 3½, I received this email from your mom:

"I just wanted to share a beautiful moment I had today with the boys. We sat with the backyard door open and watched a storm roll in and the rain flood our backyard. While we watched, William turned to me and said 'I love you, Mama.' I turned to him and said 'I love you, too' and then we hugged each other for a while. It was the first time either of the boys said 'I love you' to me. Very special. I think I will remember that moment all my life."

Lily

GEESE APPEAR HIGH OVER US,
PASS, AND THE SKY CLOSES. ABANDON,
AS IN LOVE OR SLEEP, HOLDS
THEM TO THEIR WAY, CLEAR,
IN THE ANCIENT FAITH: WHAT WE NEED
IS HERE. AND WE PRAY, NOT
FOR NEW EARTH OR HEAVEN, BUT TO BE
QUIET IN HEART, AND IN EYE
CLEAR. WHAT WE NEED IS HERE.

Wendell Berry
from "The Wild Geese"

Dear Boys,

When I was a kid, Smith's Pond saved my soul. My dog Duke was my sidekick, a thoroughbred mutt—some sort of spaniel mixed with whatever, Springer Spaniel I guessed because of his talent of jumping straight up and looking around for rabbits and pheasants at Smith's Pond. In a year he grew to forty-five pounds of white-and-black, floppy-eared, tick-collecting, field-romping primal force.

Smith's Pond was the last hint of wilderness in Suburban Philadelphia, no cute lawns and asphalt driveways. No rules either. Just cattails, mud, and murk. Duke and I lived for this. We hunted at Smith's Pond most every day after school, which was only a few blocks away.

Duke had his own agenda—snaring pheasants and rabbits. In this he was defeated daily. For my pet zoo, I lusted after the beautiful painted pond turtles sunning themselves far out on logs in the murk or giant bullfrogs lurking in the rushes at pond's edge, or the wily and huge water snakes, who could do real damage with their teeth, unlike their smaller relatives in my slithering collection.

I'd creep up on the snakes and bullfrogs, but no matter how cunning my stealth, they disappeared at the last second in a flash. I constructed a turtle trap, a semisubmersible box with a hole in the top for the turtles to fall into and then be roped to shore. But the nonchalant turtles were too smart for me.

Duke and I didn't care that we bagged nothing at Smith's Pond. I had enough reptiles and amphibians in my basement zoo already. What mattered was the pond itself—about the size of a city block. It was all ours. I never saw another kid or adult there, even though developments encroached on every side and traffic constantly roared from a highway.

Obviously the pond and everything in it were under a death sentence. Only a year after Duke and I left for other hunting grounds at our new house miles away it was plowed under, burying our marvelous friends alive without a thought. A half dozen asbestos-sided stick jobs went up with perfect patios, jolly barbecue sets, and TVs with seven channels. The taming of Penn Wynne was complete. An immense boredom settled over the town.

Boys, don't let boredom settle on you. You guys will need a taste of the wild, a place in nature where you can roam free.

Don't let suburbia close you down, and that includes a suburbia of the soul that lurks in the digital universe. Get out into the real. It's been there for millions of years. Your gut knows this. Your body longs for it. Get moving.

THE OLD PEOPLE CAME TO LOVE THE SOIL
AND SAT OR RECLINED ON THE GROUND WITH
A FEELING OF BEING CLOSE TO A MOTHERING
POWER . . . THAT IS WHY THE OLD INDIAN
STILL SITS UPON THE EARTH TO COME CLOSER
IN KINSHIP TO OTHER LIVES AROUND.
Luther Standing Bear

Dear Boys,

This is the first of several letters to you about a confounding mystery—sex. I confess up front that we know little about the subject. All knowledge is hidden in our reptilian brains, unreachable by mere humans. But I am writing about what I have experienced and what I think I know so far.

Not much.

These sex letters are then mostly about Not Knowing.

I do know one bit—sex in thought, deed and self-identity will be a huge chunk of your post-puberty life. From others you will receive a torrent of advice, preaching, and offers of an endless array of clothing, adornments, chemicals and sexual choices—hetero, homo, bi and nuances and footnotes of each, plus combos, fancies and insanities.

Ignore all that. Stick to what you know, in your heart and mind. And above all be kind to your dates, your mates and yourself.

As of now, long before you read this, you are all boy—five-year-old experts at dump trucks, excavators and tales of heroic rescues featuring kids just like yourself preparing for great manly adventures.

Same as me at five years, so I am told. Here's what happened to me in the years thereafter. Use whatever seems useful. Toss whatever seems useless.

In sixth grade, our teacher Mr. Fritz, made us memorize all of Kipling's poem "If".

"If you can force your heart and nerve and sinew

To serve your turn long after they are gone

And so hold on when there is nothing in you

Except the Will which says to them: 'Hold on' . . .

Yours is the Earth and everything that's in it

And—which is more—

You'll be a Man, my son.

But soon it seemed more complicated, this being a Man. I walked with my shoulders hunched up. That's the way football players walked. I didn't know about their shoulder pads.

Pop and the preachers were silent about sex. But in the library the boys clustered around *Popular Mechanics* and giggled at the "RUPTURED?" ads for hernia supports. Was the truss a sexual device?

At the sixth grade class picnic Sammy Mack stuck a hot dog in his fly and wiggled it in front of girls. In the halls Dirty Dee Bond (a girl!) was "giving the finger"—whatever that meant. I went to a spin-the-bottle party and kissed a girl named Alice Wilbert.

Alice told the other girls that she liked me and I courageously walked her home from school. At her door she began to cry. "What's wrong, Alice?" I asked. But she only cried harder.

The next day, playing first base, on the playground before school. I dropped a foul ball in my eye and she screeched with laughter as I lay twisting in the dust. "What an ass!" she hollered.

A girl said "ass." And I had no idea why.

That spring we studied the mating habits of the Praying Mantis. Mr. Fritz instructed us to watch while the female Mantis was serviced by the male. The boys gasped as she then turned and bit his head off.

Rumors on the playground were about "doing it" and what a girl was like down there and taking off your clothes to "do it."

I resolved never to take off my clothes with a girl. Ever.

Penn Wynne elementary school expected us to learn the adult graces in an extracurricular dance class.

Pop, in one of his rare direct religious orders—later overruled by Mom in one of her rare direct confrontations—said "no dancing class."

The mystery was just starting.

For you guys, it has started about the age when you read this. That mystery will never end. Enjoy it.

Dear Boys,

In junior high school, the gym coach, Crusty Diller, said the new seventh-grade boys would be expected to comport themselves like men. This meant push-ups, sit-ups, rope-climbing, football with tackling, and taking a shower with the other boys. Crusty wanted us to be men, and naked.

Naked? For me to be naked with other boys watching was to exhibit myself as a freak. I had changed in a way that no other boy had even begun to change. I was odd in an unspeakable area of my body. I knew it was unspeakable because in those days no adult ever spoke about it. So I broke Mr. Diller's rules, kept my underpants on at all times, and hoped he wouldn't notice that I hadn't showered.

I couldn't ask the other boys what was happening to me. They'd talk and make it worse than it was. How could I ask them what I suspected I was supposed to know already?

The boys knew other secrets too, like the meaning of "whack off" and "necking" and "making out" and how it was a great sexual conquest to discover a kid's mother's first name and then yell it across the playground: "Dorothy!" or "Black Dot!" They scored on me, and sent slips of paper around the classroom, smirking at the single, racist black spot of ink.

I acted as if I understood.

As to the act itself, I concluded it was like pissing. There'd be this cheerleader standing where the urinal was, with an ankle-length black dress that flew up to reveal orange and black school color underpants and . . . But occasional wet dreams told me that sex was not like pissing. It was something else.

I tried so hard to be a man in Crusty Diller's terms that I developed a hernia. Now I was doubly freakish: peach fuzz hair and a hernia.

Before going off to be examined for the hernia, I spent hours clipping hairs with fingernail scissors until I was sure the doctor wouldn't notice. The doctor confirmed the hernia and shouted to my mother in the next room, "My God, he's shaved his pubes!" My mother, with more manners than he, said nothing. The doctor assured me I needed an immediate operation, that it could only get worse.

I promised God that I'd do just about anything for Him if He'd fix the problem. That week I hit a grand-slam homerun during lunch-hour recess and ripped my gut so badly rounding the bases that I couldn't walk for three days. On the fourth day, the hernia was healed.

Advice: (a) learn to doubt doctors now and then, (b) from peach fuzz to full bush down there, learn to honor each hair. (c) did God fix my hernia? I have no idea. Just another cosmic wink. It's okay to believe in those winks. They happen all the time and you probably don't notice.

Dear Boys,

Once there was a thriving international outfit called Boy Scouts. Founded in 1910, Scouting enrolled over ten million boys into its ranks before a pedophilia scandal decimated it in the early 21st century. Maybe Scouting exists no more.

I miss Scouting.

I became a little kid Cub Scout in the 1940s, and soon I was a pre-teen Boy Scout, aiming to the ranks of Second Class, First Class and then Life, Star and Eagle, a climb up the ladder to Scouting glory. Eagle was a very big deal. A boy who made Eagle was saluted in the town newspaper and businesses and politicians cheered for him.

I never made Eagle, never came close. Here's why, for what you boys can make of it.

Cub Scouting was fun, fun, fun. We eight-and-nine-year-olds played in the Den Mother's backyard (dodge ball, hide-and-go seek) and fashioned ash trays from old tuna fish cans. Scouting promised fun and this was indeed fun, fun, fun.

Then we hit 11 and it all became more serious, but still promised fun unending, coupled with weighty adult matters like The Scout Oath: "On my honor I will do my best to do my duty to God and my country." At the time I thought this was a pleasant promise but now it seems that joining God and Country is not only silly, it is dangerous.

The rest of the Oath was fine with me, still is. I promised to "Help other people at all times and to keep myself physically strong, mentally awake and morally straight." "Morally straight" is a bit iffy. Are we talking no lusty thoughts or naughty words? Petty guilt looms and such guilt can reduce a lad to nervous collapse.

Then there's the Scout Law, a fine set of pronouncements: A Scout is commanded to be Trustworthy, Loyal, Helpful, Friendly, Courteous, Kind, Obedient, Cheerful, Thrifty, Brave, Clean, and Reverent.

Okay, we can dither on Clean and "traveling with a clean crowd." Are we talking frequent showers here or dirty thoughts and sex, sex, sex?

As to Reverent, when you worry about what God wants you to do you are liable to get all tangled up in fundamental biblical niceties that contradict each other and deliver you to absurd anxieties. Don't go there.

But, guys, you could do worse than the Scout Law as your guiding model. I am sure you have many more atrocious models in your day.

Scouting was also about earning Merit badges for your uniform. We paraded our badges like little generals in our pseudo-military outfits.

Some of these Merit badge skills are still helpful to me years later, such as knot tying, latrine digging, campfire cooking, compass use, home repair, wilderness survival and dozens more. Fun was not only moral, it was useful.

I felt good, doing good, being good and trooping with good people.

All that changed gradually, then suddenly.

And this is what I want to tell you about.

First of all, puberty was upon me big time. Doing "good" wasn't sexy. Girls didn't like good boys. They hungered for bad boys, tough guys. Being good began to seem a bit sissy. And dull.

Most damning of all were the evils of the scouts themselves. Our troop leader, Mr. Wisner, was a liar. Before a weekend camping trip, he lied to my father that for sure we would hold Sunday services in the woods. We didn't, and he never intended to. On the ride home he suggested that we tell my dad a little white lie, that we sang hymns, prayed etc.

Also, lustful thoughts emerged at our campsite. We sang "Lady of Spain I adore you. Pull down your pants I'll explore you."

And we smoked Kool cigarettes: Supposedly a necessary rite of manhood.

All weekend we tormented new recruits, Tenderfoots, by ordering them into the woods to find "Lefthanded Smoke Shifters" and banishing them from camp until they found the shifters, which of course did not exist.

On the way home, Mr. Wisner, always laughing at our terror, drove his station wagon at 80 mph, in a 40 mph zone.

Later that year, our troop helped out at our church's Strawberry Festival. A feature film during the festivities was "Victory at Sea." I remember vivid shots of Japanese soldiers being roasted alive by flame throwers for our enjoyment.

This was a dark side of good people that I never suspected, and a long way from fashioning ash trays from tuna fish cans.

But the end of scouting for me came suddenly when our troop shipped out for a week of tenting at Camp Delmont in Green Lake, Pennsylvania, miles from home. Here I encountered Scouts who seemed uninformed about the Scout Oath or Laws. A roving gang of city Scouts tortured me by making me wear my underpants outside my pants because I was a Camp Delmont newcomer. Day by day they hunted me through the woods to make sure I complied.

I was terrified and finally very sick. An ambulance rushed me back home with pneumonia. For weeks I lay in bed pondering this new Scouting revelation.

It was clear that for me scouting was no longer fun, fun, fun. And forget about the good boy bit.

I figured I had more important stuff to do with my life. My father had always explained that he was "Nobody important."

Hitting puberty, where you guys are now, I decided I would become "Somebody."

I quit scouting, hung up my fake military uniform with its fake military merit badges. It still hangs in some closet somewhere.

But while Scouting failed for me, as all human organizations tend to fall short of expectation, the idea of Scouting is still valuable. We *did* have fun. We *did* feel important and wanted. We loved being "Prepared" and "Doing a Good turn". And in the cold woods we learned we could survive on our own away from family, with a little help from our friends.

Boys, hold on to the Scout Oath. Honor the Scout Law. They really matter. And it turns out that good guys are sexy after all.

PAY ATTENTION!
(note posted on my office wall)

Dear Boys,

Try to understand the role of Virtue in my young life, and perhaps in yours.

In my day, doing Good was how you got into heaven, which was a real place. Doing Bad ended you in the fires of Hell. This was the common theology of many churches and the general if vague notion of society.

But Virtue also had its practical side: if you were Good you probably got rich, were elected to high office, married a swell girl, had healthy kids, a fancy car and a neat house and were the pride of your neighborhood (although Pride was a sin).

It is easy to laugh at such notions today, except for the fact that some of it is still valuable, and sort of true, if out of style.

When I was swaying in my backyard tree fort, I worshipped God in the clouds, in the sunrises and sunsets, in the stars. I prayed to Him that President Eisenhower and Comrade Khrushchev would not blow up His creation.

Meanwhile there were problems to be solved under the tree fort. That's where you had a deadly contest between good and evil, a contest I could do something about.

The oak trees were strong. I decided that they were therefore good. I also decided that they were being treated unfairly by certain faster-growing, weaker and ignoble trees, like the silver maple. Oaks grew about six inches a year, whereas the weak silver maple could do two feet or better in as much time.

I took sides. I scouted the woods for oak seedlings, and I transplanted them on the borders of our property, slashing down weeds and silver maples to make a space and let the sunlight through.

I lectured Pop about the value of strength, and as a hurricane approached, I orated to him about cutting down the huge silver maple on our front lawn. Did he admire weakness? Why couldn't he bring himself to hurt a tree? Did he doubt my judgment? Because I wasn't going to sleep in my bedroom under some silver maple during the storm. So I slept in the living room while the wind toppled trees and the power failed. But the silver maple survived.

There were good and bad animals under my fort. Predators, like foxes and crows, were evil—and those they preyed on, such as rabbits and pheasants, were good. In the junior-high print shop I worked up bold posters that proclaimed NO HUNTING and under that PREDATOR HUNTING IS OK, and I signed them: "The Henderson Game Commission."

I learned about Ben Franklin's virtue chart in a Personal Growth leaflet sent to me from the Government Printing Office in Washington, D.C. It was one of dozens of leaflets I ordered from a catalogue that included titles like *Ten Ways to Become A Winning Public Speaker* and *You and Your Teeth*.

I found that many of my virtues were the same ones Ben Franklin was interested in, and, like him, I expected practical results. I also expected that someday my biographers would be interested in my chart. At Franklin's suggestion, I marked myself every night with pluses and minuses and totaled up the score in the various virtues at the end of each week. I did best in Moderation, Loyalty, Non-Boasting, Justice, and Industry, and not so good in Tranquility.

It was from Ben Franklin that I learned about a virtue I'd never thought of before.

Meditation.

Meditation was an important virtue, and I took care of it each night in a window alcove off my bedroom that I had turned into a meditation chamber. The alcove was just big enough for an old kitchen table, a chair, and me. I strung a wire and hung a sheet across the alcove entrance to shield it from the bedroom I shared with brother Bob.

Bob said nothing, as he watched the closed curtain. To me, Bob 16 months younger was a shadowy annoyance whom I would meet as a true, beloved friend only years later.

In order to score proper marks in Meditation I had to read at least one Personal Growth leaflet and a chapter from the Bible each night, plus enter my ratings on my Virtue Chart. After that, I would turn out the light, open the window no matter how cold the weather, and gaze at the stars. I knew God was out there. I would reach out to the sky to touch Him. I expected that one night He would touch me back.

It was in this alcove that I quite by accident discovered another virtue. I noticed I could produce the most remarkable feelings, actually transport myself into ecstasy, with attention to my crotch. I hadn't imagined that my body could feel as wonderful as this, so transfixed.

It had to be a sin. Didn't the Bible say so somewhere?

Each week I graded myself worse and worse in a category I called "SD" (a meaningless code for what I was trying not to do. I didn't want my biographers to know my shame). I listed this virtue, SD, under the general heading of Bodily Clean, a class of virtues that included a bath on Monday, Wednesday, and Saturday; clean toenails and fingernails; three full glasses of water a day, and combing my hair.

I became so upset with flunking SD that I flunked myself in the entire Virtue Chart at each week's end. But I couldn't give up the chart, I thought, because I had to grade myself. I didn't trust anybody else's grades—not the church's, not the school's.

Each night I would climb into bed and pray in despair that God would help me stop. And then I asked him to bless Mom and Pop and Bob and Ruth and President Eisenhower.

Boys, a Virtue Chart is a good idea. But don't chastise yourself for flunking now and then. Do Pay Attention—that's the main virtue. And leave self-pleasure off the chart. You will flunk often and drive yourself looney-tunes in guilt.

ORIGEN
"Eunuchs for the Kingdom of God."
Matthew 19:12

The leaping cheerleaders
Were driving me crazy,
Origen.

In Sunday School I heard
You knocked off your gonads
For God.

What I needed to know was
How to proceed?

A razor?
A knife?
A rope on a slammed
Door knob?

YOU DO NOT HAVE TO BE GOOD.
YOU DO NOT HAVE TO WALK ON YOUR KNEES
FOR A HUNDRED MILES THROUGH THE DESERT,
REPENTING.
YOU ONLY HAVE TO LET THE SOFT ANIMAL
OF YOUR BODY
LOVE WHAT IT LOVES.
Mary Oliver

Dear Boys,

You will meet all sorts of teachers, in your school year. Some boring, most ok, and few fabulous. Earlier I sketched out some of my elementary school teachers. Here is the account of one crazy guy who ruled our junior high school with a whistle and a fat bounce.

Dogs were an obsession for principal, Edward Holyoke Snow. To him life was a dogfight. Snow's favorite slogan, which the entire school—teachers included—was required to chant at pep rallies was, "It's not the size of the dog in the fight, it's the size of the fight in the dog."

Snow prowled the halls, a six-foot, 300-pound, crew-cut, bulldog-jawed fellow in school-colored orange and black socks and tie, his silver whistle swinging from his neck.

The whistle was Snow's gun. By fondling it in a noisy school assembly or by pointing it at a misbehaving kid, he would get instant obedience. And when he actually blew it, followed by his outraged bellow, students shivered and the object of his noise cringed and awaited his judgment. Snow's whistle was no respecter of child, teacher, or God—he'd

even blow it in the halls during the morning devo-
tion period, showing a discourtesy to God that I
wondered about and then hastily forgot. One didn't
question Ed Snow.

Ed Snow rehearsed us in his dog-inspired war
games by assembling his troops in the auditorium for
any excuse and haranguing us on the evils of tight
pants and Duck's Ass haircuts; on the glories of
Roger Bannister's first mile run in less than four
minutes; on obliterating our rival, Upper Darby
Junior High School, in every sport.

Snow's Ardmore Junior High School Handbook
was my first experience with secular philosophy. It
was issued in a new edition each year and included
everything I was told that I needed to know, from the
specific ("All eating is to be done in the cafeteria") to
the cosmic: "On the plains of desolation bleach the
bones of countless millions who at the moment of
victory sat down to rest and resting died." Or myste-
riously, "All but the dead left the field."

Real men must win the dogfight of life, and they
will if they don't give up. Communism, lying, cowardice, cheating, sneakiness, and sex were bad. He
stalked school dances and forbade close dancing.

Snow was quite open about his sex phobia. As a
prize for drumming up the most magazine subscrip-

tions for his War Memorial College Scholarship Fund, he bused the top-ten sellers (I was third) to the movie *Battle Cry.*

Unfortunately, he hadn't seen the movie and didn't know that some scenes took place in a whorehouse. I thought they were just friendly ladies. Snow apologized to the school and advised that we boycott the movie.

I will take a Snow over a boring teacher any day. If you kids find yourself saddled with a dull teacher, try a bit of daydreaming, take secret notes in class on your daydreams, jot poetry. When I taught kids at Staten Island Academy for a year after dropping out of boring Harvard Graduate School, I tried to make each class interesting and funny. We kids were in this together. No exhausted adults allowed.

Dear Boys,

After you hit your teen years and beyond you may find yourself on an endless quest to figure out the cosmos for yourself, rejecting the advice of your parents and pontificating grandparents like myself. Your search will be hard, and worth it. Don't despair and above all don't seek comfort in booze or drugs. No answers there, only fake comfort and disaster.

In a way, the quest *is* the answer. Don't let it become mere confusion.

What you may come up with years later is simple wonder. Wonder is enough I figure. Love and wonder.

Here is an account of my own teen questing, a flailing about which ended decades later with love and wonder.

During my sophomore year in high school, Carol, a classmate, and I began telephone conversations on "deep" subjects that most other kids avoided. Every night we argued about poetry, philosophy and music.

We figured kids like us should stick together. So we formed an exclusive club, the Main Line Philosophy Club, Carol and I and a half-dozen other boys. (They may have arrived expecting sexual favors from Carol, who was rumored to let herself be "felt up.")

The existence or nonexistence of God was often our topic week after week. Now and then we touched on Communism and ethics. But what we wanted to settle was Was He or Wasn't He.

Sprawled on Carol's living-room floor, we scored points, often not assessing arguments so much as the lack of intelligence of the speaker.

"You just fell ten points on my list," a class brain informed me after I'd defended God's existence with a quote from the *Reader's Digest*.

Some of them dropped Hegel, Marx, and Wittgenstein into the debate. I doubt if they had read the books, but to protect myself against my ignorance of philosophers I hadn't read I bought a paperback titled *Philosophy Made Simple*. It outlined dozens of thinkers in a few paragraphs each. When confronted, I'd excuse myself to another room, check out *Philosophy Made Simple*, and then rush back with a retort.

Most of the kids proclaimed themselves to be agnostics and a few said they were atheists. I alone defended God's certain existence with my six points, the best of which was oddly the last one:

6) Only God could have thought up the odd plan of Christ dying on the cross. That perfection should die in torture must be God's idea.

Anyway, the Philosophy Club argued and argued about the existence of God until we argued ourselves blue. One kid brought a six-pack of beer and told us he'd rather stay high all day than think. We played records and danced.

Young Life, an evangelical youth group, heard about us and concluded the Club required conversion. We were invited to a face-to-face confrontation by the Young Life leader, who would speak for Jesus, whereas a boy named Gay Wilson, a straight-A math student who had scored early acceptance at MIT, would defend God's nonexistence.

Here's what Gay said—boiled down to his six points:

1) There is no God because the emotions of religion can be removed from the brain by depriving it of certain chemicals.

2) Everything in the universe that exists can be proven to exist. Not so with God.

3) The search for God is just a father hunt.

4) If God exists, why is there so much misery in the world?

5) Man is even now creating a virus and soon will make soulless, intelligent life.

6) Since the universe has always existed, there is no need to think about a Creator.

From the sidelines, I shouted out refutations. (Imagine the universe always existing! The magnitude of this new idea stumped me.) But I was growing tired of my own six points. I was growing tired of the Philosophy Club.

So I thought up a new club, the Thoreau Club.

We'd assemble in a small room at the very top of the high school. The Thoreau Club would be limited to those who *really* understood. But I never made it very clear to myself or anybody else what it was that we would really understand.

* * *

After one of my regular anti-church sermons at the dinner table, Pop said, "Bill, why don't you go out for track again? You were happier when you ran the quarter-mile."

I dove off my chair and announced my most recent theory from the dining-room rug. "Happiness isn't the point! Rationality is! What did God give us our brains for but to use, Pop!"

Logic was my path to the Truth, and it was also the key to society's organization. I wrote in my journal: "Citizens must be smart to be logical. Therefore, sterilize all men and women with an IQ under 110. This is one way, if not *the* way, to produce a truly free society not dominated by dictators, the church, or Madison Avenue." Ghastly notion.

As founder and editor-in-chief of the school newspaper, *The Forum*, I proclaimed the New Age of Reason. I wrote: "The New Age has dawned. The sunlight of a new generation of youth is about to flood the landscape of wars and disease, jealousies and hypocrisies. We will have no dogma. We will abolish instinct and mass stupidity by the reasoning of the new youth."

As to my role in the New Age of Reason, I mused in my journal: "Could I possibly be the bit of dust to realize the dreams of thousands of pain- and hunger-stricken men? Could I move this mountain? The thought terrifies me. But I will try. My God, I will try until I drop dead!"

Meanwhile, I no longer stuck "In Jesus' name" on to the end of my nightly prayers. But that was just more Reason. I believed in a God of all religions, not just Jesus' God.

More significantly, I didn't open the alcove window at night and reach out to God in the stars.

Instead, I lay flat on my back in bed and thrust my hand to the ceiling. I figured if God was God, He would find me here.

Only once did I lose it all.

Maybe God really *was not*. I'd never thought about it seriously. But now I did. He didn't exist, and neither did Truth.

"How bored you'd be if you ever found Truth. What else would there be to do . . . and besides maybe Truth is just a personal thing."

If that was so, then I was out of a job as a future prophet. Billions of personal ideas must be tolerated. "O Compassion," I scribbled, with more despair than compassion.

I woke up at night horrified.

But after a week of this, I suddenly realized the fault of atheism. It was irrational. It wasn't *getting* me anywhere.

What was the *use* of it all.

None.

Having solved that problem, I began to marvel at what other kids knew, for instance Carol's friend Tad, who once worked in a hospital and had seen real death.

I wrote: "August 16, 1959. Tad and I talked about death. When you are dying the mouth suddenly goes limp like a fish's mouth; then the eyes, which may have been staring in terror, continue to stare but slowly glaze over. Then you are dead."

* * *

Advice: Our current digital age of speedy and shallow opinions is not going to make it easy for you guys to get a footing. In the Philosophy Club we had time to bat ideas around, however ridiculous and depressing.

Slow down. Make room for love and wonder.

Despair is not an option.

Here is another reason to own a dog.

In *Dog Years*, Mark Doty recalls moments with his beloved Mr. Beau:

"When I adopted him, he was a neglected slip of a thing, but his heart was capable of soaring. I call on his spirit when things get logy, when I feel an internal clock slipping into what Dickinson called an "hour of lead." Attention to the mortal shadowing of all beauty—that's a perspective that comes to me too easily, something I have to resist. And that's why I loved that heavy golden paw tapping at my knee—notice me, come back. A kind of sweet slap, with the blunt tips of his nails poking at me. A slap I miss now with all my heart."

Dear Boys,

As I moved deeper into my teen years, this business of being a male, brought on agonized thinking.

I tried to find the basic psychological premises for a love affair: "Be nice, but don't get so mushy and girl-like—be a man, you know, *tough*," I scribbled in my journal.

"Don't let a woman get away with anything. No weakness," I quoted the advice of a classmate.

I contrived elaborate plans for wooing a girl—watching her, studying her interests and her reactions to other boys, plotting to meet her needs. But none of these ever worked.

"Try a little tenderness." I got that from a popular song, and it forced me into a reversal from my be-tough period. I tried to exhibit powerful indications of tenderness. It didn't work so hot, either.

Then I learned from Will Durant's *Story of Philosophy* that Schopenhauer doubted the use of the entire effort: "Love is a deception practiced by nature to cover up reproduction." I copied this wisdom into my journal.

I tried my mainstay—the Bible, the place where Pop's guidance had its source. First Corinthians 16, verse 13, said: "Watch ye, stand fast in the faith and quit you like men." Since my opinion of the faith was less enthusiastic now, all that was left to me was quitting myself like a man, whatever quitting meant.

But then I read where Emerson said "To be a man, you must be a nonconformist," so I wrote an essay attacking the shallow beliefs of contemporary Christians, and read it aloud in school.

Pop didn't know what to say about my manly anti-church nonconformity. But I did. I said: "Pop, people don't respect a man who doesn't stand up for his own ideals."

I expected that lots and lots of girls were going to be impressed by the new Emersonian me. Except they weren't, not a one.

"The diamond cannot be polished without friction, nor the man perfected without trial." It was an old Chinese proverb. I wrote it on a slip of paper and carried it around in my wallet. I would refer to it every once in a while and keep my courage up.

Perhaps you boys will have a slogan in your wallet to keep up your courage. Keep the slogan simple. "Love and wonder" works for me. "Shut the fuck up!" does nicely to banish self doubts, if that slogan fails.

WHAT IS LIFE?
IT IS THE FLASH OF A FIREFLY IN THE NIGHT.
IT IS THE BREATH OF A BUFFALO IN THE WINTER
TIME.
IT IS THE LITTLE SHADOW THAT RUNS
ACROSS THE GRASS AND LOSES ITSELF IN THE SUNSET.
Crowfoot, orator of the Blackfoot Nation

Dear Boys,

And then of course having mingled with girls for years in class and on the playground, you pick somebody special and with vast trepidation you ask her to do something special, just the two of you.

Edie Osborn was the target of my first age 13 request, a pretty, popular, friendly girl sort of a "trophy date," who seemed unlikely to laugh at my blurting suggestion. (The blurt is a good idea. Admit to yourself that you are nervous and use your nerves. Just spit it out. "I thought a movie Saturday night?" It's a huge leap into the sexual wilderness. Be nervous).

Edie said, "ok"

In silence, Pop drove me to our date. He parked outside of Edie's house and I rang the doorbell and met her parents and Edie got in the car between Pop and me and shook hands with Pop. We drove to the Suburban Theater to see *The House of Wax* in 3-D. After we put on our special glasses, I reached my arm around her chair. Edie leaned forward. I acted as if I didn't notice her leaning. We watched a woman stripped and encased in hot wax. She became a wax statue. Edie leaned forward until the movie was over.

I called Pop to come and pick us up, and while we were waiting outside I tried a joke.

"Let's get married," I said.

Edie laughed.

I interpreted this as my first achievement with a girl. So I said it again, and Edie laughed again, only this time not so loud. The third time Edie looked bored and stared down the road for her ride home, and when it came, we got in the car, I walked her to the door, and then Pop and I drove home in silence.

Edie asked me to a party at another girl's house. Both Edie and the girl were said to be pretty and popular, so I accepted. It was important to me that a girl have a reputation as pretty and popular.

I didn't understand what made a girl pretty. Being blonde like Marilyn Monroe might. If the boys said a girl was pretty, I accepted that, even if she was decorated with pimples and braces.

And if she was a cheerleader or a class officer, then she was popular. To have a cheerleader nod to me in the hall was to have a good day; to have her stop to talk with me was to be destined for greatness.

Edie was class secretary.

After she invited me to the party, it got around that we were going steady. I liked that rumor. It proved I was becoming popular, and wasn't that what girls were for? To make you popular? It was all part of the grading system. Maybe even of the Permanent Record itself. God, my parents, teachers, and other kids were watching me, and I was doing just fine because Edie invited me to the party.

At the party, my eyes teared when I tried to talk. All of the other couples disappeared into the two cars parked in the garage. Word drifted back that they were making out.

Edie and I sat alone in the rec room reading magazines. I wondered if I was supposed to ask her to make out, and how I'd ask that, and what you did if you were making out.

But she never asked me to another party and the rumors about us stopped and for a time I didn't have to worry about making out.

I had faith that if I worked hard, got A's and B's, was elected to some class office, did extracurricular work, and struggled to succeed at the hernia-threatening quarter mile for the track team, a girl would be mine, a really popular, really pretty girl.

The key was to be really, really good.

It's not hard to figure out where I got these practical notions of what a girlfriend was for. Such notions surround us. Resist, resist. People are not <u>For</u> anything but your caring for them. Be a rebel. Buck the system.

Dear Boys,

We live in a age that is mad for celebrities, or influencers as they are currently dubbed. People look to these icons for advice on how to live, act, dress and then ditch them for the next icon.

May I suggest to you a better celebrity, one that will last you for a lifetime: St. Francis, born 1081 in Assisi, Italy. His dad was a wealthy clothes merchant and Francis lived his youth as a playboy and would-be knight until rejecting his dad. He embraced a primitive Christianity and attempted to walk in Christ's exact footprints. He cared not much for the Old Testament and everything for the New. To him, all that is required of us is a recognition of God's love and a constant meditation on that love. The ponderings of theologians were worthless.

Power—any domination by one person of another, however subtle—is anathema. Thus his followers became not an order, but a brotherhood, without leaders. No one was more important than another, and Francis considered himself the least of the least.

Francis preached that money was dirty. He refused to carry it or touch it; it inspired in him an almost physical revulsion. One day a follower left a bag of money. A brother picked it up—perhaps it could be donated to the poor? Francis scolded him and forced him to bury the sack in donkey dung.

The same for property—Jesus owned nothing, neither should the brothers. Books, which were expensive, were banned, the Bible excepted. One might accumulate many books and pride oneself on a library, or on the false learning that books inspired.

To his sexually libertine neighbors and some priests and monks, Francis preached a strict chastity: all passion for God.

Permanent housing was forbidden. His brothers should live in temporary reed shelters, or a cave would do, or a room donated from someone outside the flock. "If we owned anything we should have to have weapons to protect ourselves . . . we are resolved to possess nothing temporal in this world."

What really resonates in our memory is that Sunday School illustration of St. Francis and the animals. He adored animals. It is said that animals recognized him as a saint before people did, and that they fled to him for refuge because they sensed that with him human wickedness couldn't touch them; that a hunted rabbit curled up against him; that birds perched on his shoulders and listened to his sermons;

that the vicious wolf terrifying the town of Gubbio
was tamed by his gentle words.

But we remember him as one of the few people
in Church history who loved all living beings without reservation, who followed Christ simply, without
petty theology. And we adore him, too, for his former libertinism and frenzy for renown. We know
Francis in our own time and person. No plaster saint
this. He lives today as he lived eight hundred years
ago.

It would take 46 billion years to reach the observable edge of the universe if you travel at the speed of light, which is 186,000 miles per second.
BH/Journal

I DO NOT THINK IT IS IMPORTANT
WHETHER A MAN ENTERS RELIGION
BY THE FRONT DOOR OR THE BACK
DOOR, AS LONG AS HE ENTERS . . .
IF WE CAN ARRIVE AT A POSITION
IN WHICH JESUS ADMIRED THE
LILIES OF THE VALLEY AND ST.
FRANCIS LOVED THE BIRDS AS
GOD'S OWN CREATURES, WE HAVE
STUMBLED UPON THE VERY
SOURCE FROM WHICH ALL
RELIGIONS TOOK THEIR RISE.
Lin Yutang

I had spent the evening in a great city, with two friends, reading and discussing poetry and philosophy. We parted at midnight. I had a long drive in a hansom to my lodging. . . . All at once, without warning of any kind, I found myself wrapped in a flame-colored cloud. For an instant I thought of fire, an immense conflagration somewhere close by in that great city; the next, I knew that the fire was within myself. Directly afterward there came upon me a sense of exaltation, of immense joyousness accompanied or immediately followed by an intellectual illumination impossible to describe. Among other things, I did not merely come to believe, but I saw that the universe is not composed of dead matter, but is, on the contrary, a living Presence.

Dr. H. M. Bucke (1902)

Dear Boys,

I know that your years may be very different from my own. Certainly they will differ from the years of our common forebearer. Let's call him The Ancestor.

About this Ancestor we know next to nothing. My dad, Pop, didn't think anybody would be interested in himself or where he came from. But about The Ancestor he did recall a family legend that long ago in the mid-1860's his dad's father, (name unknown) was shot in the Civil War. (We assume he fought for the North.) A stranger dragged him to a nameless stream in a nameless state bathed his wounds, saved his life. That wounded man, your great, great, great grandfather—The Ancestor— survived from a small act of kindness.

You exist because of that small act.

But this letter is not about the Ancestor. It is about small acts that have huge results. Usually nobody notices at first that anything much has happened. Only later do you discover that a little word or deed has huge consequences for your life.

There have been many small acts of kindness from many people in my 80 plus years. A stranger handed me her umbrella as I stood in a torrential rain grieving a relative's cancer diagnosis; a renowned college lecturer who looked me in the eye for a nano-second and by his gaze assured the bewildered sophomore that I would be ok; and most important a friend's remark to me while I was flailing about campus desperate for answers: "It all depends if you think life is sacred or not."

That statement, forgotten by him, was the rock on which I eventually built my life. Of course life is sacred! Why else keep trying to figure it out? Start there. Sacred. Even if you go nowhere else that's where you begin.

The same for The Ancestor. A passing moment of kindness, for a wounded stranger and the result, you two!

Pay attention. The essence may be in the small stuff. And particularly in the small stuff you do for other people. You may never know how your good travels. Even a hundred years from now your little kindness may make big changes for the better.

Dear Boys,

Dogs have always been an essential partner for me.

In Ted Kerasote's memoir *Merle's Door*, about his rescue dog Merle he remembers their last year together: I can't read this without choking up.

I put some country-western music on the CD player and tapped my chest with my palms, he'd stand on his hind legs, put his front paws on my shoulders, and we'd dance around the great room together while he panted, "This is fun!" Sometimes, he'd even come and find me if some bluegrass music began to play on the radio, jumping off the dedicated quadruped couch, trotting into the office, wagging his tail, and pumping his paws up and down, indicating, "Let's dance.!"

* * *

I . . . walked to his grave, where I stood, listening to the hum of the river and feeling the universe still pressed out to its farthest corners by him. And I couldn't tell if the bigness was him or how we had filled each other's hearts.

Looking down I imagined him lying on his green bed. Even though he would now always be close, it seemed like too confined an end for a dog who liked to roam. I needn't have worried. When I looked up, he was bounding across the grass toward me, already as much starlight as dog. Tail lashing, front paws dancing, he twirled before me.

"You dance, Sir!" I cried.

"Ha-ha-ha!" he panted. "I dance! I DANCE!"

Dear Boys,

What do we mean when we say God?

What if He has a tattoo that says "Mother"? What if He's gay, bisexual, or nonsexual? What if He's a Wall Street WASP? A woman? What if He's short and Black?

I saw such a divinity once in high school and that's what he was, not so handsome. His name was Father Divine and he ran a church in Philadelphia with his wife, Mother Divine. Father Divine was Black and old; his wife was young and White. His congregation was of all races and ages, and they adored him.

In 1958, I visited Father Divine's church to write a high school class paper on him and his movement, which was very popular and politically significant in the Philadelphia of the 1950s. His followers numbered in the many thousands.

Food was free at the Divine church, and I sat down in a large hall with dozens of people at many rows of tables. We were fed well; heaps of mashed potatoes, chicken, and vegetables. We sat and waited for God to appear. Father Divine kept us waiting.

Finally, to a standing ovation, he entered the room with Mother Divine right behind him, and simply sat down and smiled. Said nothing. Never opened his mouth or said a word. Mother Divine did the same. They didn't eat. They didn't preach. They allowed themselves to be adored.

Father Divine was bald and dumpy, dressed in a too-tight sports jacket and about as plain a fellow as you could imagine. But he said he was God, and many believed him. To his followers, his physical appearance, including his race, meant nothing whatsoever, even as Mother Divine's sex and color were of little consequence to her flock.

To me, a sixteen-year-old recent convert to philosophy (Nietzsche, Schopenhauer, and so forth), he was of interest only as the subject of an English paper. Years later, I wondered why any of us really want to see the physical God or Jesus. What sort of curiosity is this? Does it make any difference whatsoever that Jesus becomes flesh yet again? Isn't it of far more significance that He lives with us every day as the unconditional spirit of love that we know He is?

Dear Boys,

Nothing in my eighty plus years has been harder than surviving puberty. As you perhaps have discovered, you try to figure it all out at the same time that you twist your jockey shorts to impress girls and end up as a clown. The whole business is a misery.

Years before I hit puberty, or it hit me, at Oak Park Fourth Presbyterian Church Mom and Pop bought me a ten-dollar membership in the I Am His Society. I received an embossed certificate announcing that I had been admitted into a Special Society of the Saved, a society dedicated to lifetime missionary work for Christ. I also got a thin silver ring inscribed with the initials IAH.

I put the ring in my dresser drawer and forgot about it. But in the summer of tenth grade in Ocean City, New Jersey, just after being hired as a boardwalk hot-dog slinger at Mike's Hole in the Wall luncheonette, I found the ring and put it on.

It's not that the ring had some religious significance for me. What it had was something else that I wanted—something solid, to remind me not of Him, but of Me. It became the Ring of Myself. When my eyes watered and my voice shook, I would look down at that ring through the tears. I'd see it, and it would remind me never to stop believing in me. To be strong. To buck up. Because I was having trouble remembering who I was. Lots of trouble.

I realized it was impossible for me ever to turn entirely from the church. I would never do such a thing. Of course! In fact, I still walked on the beach at dawn with my mutt Duke delivering sermons. "Don't ever forget God!" I yelled at the ocean. "No matter what happens!" I pounded my fist into my palm. Duke cocked his head, worried. He was the only one I could talk to.

Around Labor Day, a girl from school saw me cooking hot dogs at Mike's. She sat down at a stool to ask me how my summer had been.

"I am tearing down truth block by block, and I'll build it up again the same way," I bragged.

"That's nice," she smiled, deflating me.

What confidence I didn't get by looking at the Ring of Myself I tried to achieve in high school power games. I applied for and was named drum major of the Lower Merion High School All-Boy Marching Band. In my maroon-and-white drum major's uniform with the gold braid and trim and the three-foot-high fake white rabbit fur hat, I took up my position at the head of the band. With a whistle blast, I announced the start of the half-time football show. That was power. Then I'd shout and do some fancy gestures with my big silver baton. As thousands of Saturday fans watched, I led the band downfield with a determined and flamboyant duck-footed strut. But the girls were unimpressed.

I was so busy being a powerful person that I worried about neglecting my truth search. With real agony, I wondered, "Would Christ have worn a fake rabbit fur hat?"

Boys, beware of fake hats. Fake anything does not impress.

PUBERTY

Late 1940's
Peach fuzz wonder
Fishing with Pop
On Great Egg Harbor,
Ocean City, N.J.

I spear live minnows
On my hooks, right up
Through their tiny backs.
They scream in voices
I can't hear,
Don't care anyway,
Because minnows
Catch flounders.

Pop,
At the boat's bow,
Uses frozen clam bait,
Won't hurt living beings,

Any at all,
Won't prune a tree.
Catches no flounders.

Wishy washy
I laugh at him.
Flounder King, I am.
Pubic Master of the Seas.

Now,
Master of not much.
I want to scramble to
Gentle Pop
At the bow
But he has drifted away.

When my neighbor's little mutt fell through the ice in Napeague Harbor and drowned, Randy wrapped his tiny frozen body in a towel and dug a grave in his backyard. Neighbors gathered to say goodbye and dropped the petals of white lillies on his corpse. At the end of the ceremony he was all flowers.

BH/Journal

Dear Boys,

I am always amazed, indeed shocked, about how much your mom Lily is so similar to my mother, your great-grandmother Dorothy Galloway Henderson.

Dorothy was a woman of calm and decency. I never heard her say a mean word about anybody (well, maybe a few choice ones about our neighbor Mr. Coff who dug up a dozen of her Peony bushes, claiming falsely that they were on his property and comments about evangelist Oral Roberts and his faith healing racket that snared my father).

Mom's strength was constant. She helped her three children face childhood illness with compassion and intelligence. As a church leader, a deacon, she had no problem allowing her kids to attend elementary school dance classes when my father cited religious objections.

She was, like Lily, the heart of caring, compassion and calm.

At her death all of her goodness was apparent. And as I grow into old age, her dying is an example of courage to me. In 1968, she had a radical mastectomy of her right breast. When the cancer recurred, her doctors controlled it with hormones. But by early 1980 it had spread to her other breast, one lung, her liver, some bones. Her surgical scar, which they had radiated, had never healed and was infected to the rib. The doctors tried chemotherapy. Pneumonia developed.

Our family doctor said, "We can only let her die in her own way, in her own time." He added, "I love her."

Unable to walk, she was carried into Bryn Mawr Hospital by Bob, who had stayed near her and nursed her for all of her final years, while raising a family of his own.

From August 10 to September 5, 1980, from early morning to late at night, her children took turns sitting by her bedside. I wrote notes on scraps of paper, hoping that she wouldn't notice. I wanted to pretend that this was just another of her many hospital stays.

We all knew better, including Mom. "Dying is no joke," she said. But she didn't know how to quit. Usually too weak to reach her hand to her face, she never stopped trying to feed herself, even laughing when I awkwardly attempted to help "Feed the baby."

Despite her helplessness, she smiled at every guest, tried to touch them, and murmured a few words of conversation. On one of his visits, the minister announced: "Dorothy, you are going on a great adventure. It is a glorious time for you." She seemed to be unconscious, but a burp escaped her lips. "Excuse me," she smiled, and slept again.

She believed in that heavenly adventure. "I'm going to find Daddy," she said.

"We miss Daddy," Ruth said.

"We'll all be together again."

In answer to our constant questions about her occasional pain and her comfort, she often replied, "I just want you kids to get some rest and peace and quiet."

Earlier in our lives, such altruism, such self-effacement, had angered me. She was constantly giving and giving to her children, to her husband, to other people, to God. Didn't she crave a life of her own? I wanted her to be colorful, flamboyant, intellectually curious, even a bit selfish. Now at her bedside, I couldn't imagine the attraction to me of anything but her patience, her love, and her grace in living and dying. If belief in God makes such a person, then I would try hard to believe, I promised my agnostic self.

For the twelve years that she struggled with cancer, I had been working up nerve to tell her that I loved her, that in her own quiet way she was an extraordinary woman, that I was sorry that our life together was drifting away. But such outbursts of affection were unusual in our family, and I worried that I'd alarm her by implying that I knew of some crisis in her disease. Instead I dedicated a Pushcart Prize anthology to her and limited my expressions of love to a kiss before and after my visits to the hospital. Now, alone with her one afternoon, I blurted out, "I love you, Mom. You're a great mother. One of the greatest in the world." She squeezed my hand. She had heard me. I had managed to say those simple words.

Bob, Ruth, and I held her hands constantly. We all seemed to be making up for a lifetime of with-held hand holding. Each evening, before the night nurse arrived, we kissed her goodnight. Bob would bend his cheek to her lips so that she might feel she kissed him back.

When she opened her eyes in the morning, she was surrounded by photographs of Bob's and Ruth's children, and by their watercolored and crayoned drawings taped to the walls and TV screen. During the day, one of us or all of us would read Bible passages to her, or play tapes of recent Bryn Mawr Presbyterian Church services.

Two weeks before her death, the doctors said they were starting morphine injections. I was terrified that the morphine would erase her mind. I made a final appeal for her approval. Her divorced, childless son was getting married again, I told her. I planned to have a family with Genie. A baby was coming, I hoped. Earlier, I had held a *Philadelphia Inquirer* review of a Pushcart Press book over her bed, trying to convince her again that my life hadn't been a total waste, that she hadn't been in error in giving birth to me and raising me. She didn't comment. What was a small press next to a home and family, I thought she thought.

She hallucinated about ascending. "They need to repair the elevators." "I'm catching a plane tonight at seven-thirty."

She asked Ruth, "When was I born?"

Ruth told her, "November twenty-fourth, 1906."

Silence. "And when did I die?"

Later, Mom asked me to telephone Bob at work with the message that she had died at one-thirty that afternoon. She wanted to keep him informed.

"I'm so confused," she said. I told her to enjoy her visions.

Just when I despaired that I had lost her forever in fantasy, she woke and asked me if I had a clean shirt for an appointment in New York. When I returned from the appointment, she whispered that she hoped

I had had a good trip, and she imagined we should begin buying fabric for my bride's wedding dress.

Every week the doctors predicted she had only a few days to live. But then she would seem stronger. Once, sitting by her bed and thinking that she would never move again, I felt her hand on my forehead. "What are you dreaming?" she smiled.

Now as the nurses bathed her, I saw her body for the first time, how handsome and strong it still was, even though the flesh hung from useless muscles. I was reminded of her 1924 West Philadelphia High School for Girls yearbook photo, of the dark-haired, dark-eyed hockey player with the soft, determined smile. With similar determination, even as she died, the IV wounds on her arms scabbed and healed.

I took the minister aside in the hall and told him I wanted fresh funeral words about a real person, not a canned ceremony of platitudes.

Words about that girl, the hockey player. (Member of The Owl Club, The English Club, The Honor Society, and The Captain Ball Team. Named Best Mathematician. Favorite adage, "Oh gee!") Words about her teaching school to farm kids who were older and bigger than she in Troy, Pennsylvania, after graduation from the University of Pennsylvania in 1927. (Salary: $1,400 a year,

$9 a week for room and board, $25 a month saved at the Troy Building and Loan Society.) Words about a mother who held together a family of difficult children and a shy, God soaked husband; who went back to teaching high school math to put her kids through college (who endured her eldest son's pompous taunts about her coaching the cheerleading squad—"so silly, cheering for what?"); who retired to tutoring, church work, visits to invalids for Meals on Wheels, Lawrence Welk on TV, and bridge with friends. Words about a woman who lived alone in a burglar-alarmed house in a suddenly unsafe, drug-happy suburbia, who lived alone with cancer for twelve years and never complained, not once, about God, fate or discomfort.

The minister didn't have time for all of these words, so I directed him to one idea about her: a grand optimism about eternal life. He should fit the facts around that.

The minister promised "a rally for eternal life."

Mom didn't really care what kind of funeral she was given. She was a deacon in the church, but her religion wasn't one of theological niceties. Ruth, who had converted to Judaism when she married her Jewish husband, asked her what services she wanted.

"Whatever you and your Jewish faith want to give me," she said.

On September 5, 1980 she lay in a semi-coma and groaned. The nurses had just used an aspirator to clear her congested lungs, a vacuuming that left her choking and gasping to the last of her strength. I was horrified that she might be in pain and unable to tell us. "Just move your finger if it hurts," I urged. I considered covering her nose and mouth and smothering her. I begged the family doctor to increase the amount and frequency of the morphine. "I just want her out," I said. He agreed.

The morphine had the reverse effect, shocking her into a final rally. Suddenly her eyes were wide open and clear. "I want to go to the beauty parlor," she demanded.

"The beauty parlor?" I asked.

"Yes. Let's go."

Only patches of her white hair were left after the chemotherapy, but I diligently combed what was left, pretending that we were at the parlor and that I was the hairdresser. For other props, I found a can of talcum by her bed and powdered her forehead, cheeks and hair. I combed and combed, hoping she'd believe that she was at her usual Friday afternoon appointment.

She shut her eyes and seemed to enjoy it.

Then she was awake again. "I want to go home."

"Are you sure?"

"Positive!" she almost shouted, grabbing my head with her hands. "I want to go home with you!"

I telephoned the family doctor and he said it was possible to take her home, but that she might die sooner. Since it was her final wish, we decided to move her anyway. I planned a crazy scenario, Mom and her children in the back yard, listening to music, drinking some wine—she permitted herself a glass of sherry after tea total Pop died—and watching the September sky, easing her into death.

Tomorrow we'd do that.

I propped her in bed and opened the venetian blinds. We watched the sun go down together. She dozed.

On a scrap of paper cupped in my hand, I wrote, "Such incredible rebound power . . ."

"What's that? What are you writing?" she awoke suddenly and snapped, glaring at me.

"Nothing, Mom. It's nothing."

"Give me that," she ordered, and actually reached out to grab the paper.

I refused. "I'm just writing down what you say. I want people to know what a great person you are."

She sighed and lay back. Resigned to my note-taking and book-making? Happy? Angry? I'd never know.

Two nurses came to change her chest dressing. She greeted them with her arms out and grasped their hands. "Hello, how are you?" she smiled, delighted to see them, adoring them like old friends.

These were her last words.

I left the room for a few minutes and when I returned she had been treated with the aspirator and was nearly unconscious.

Because I was so sure she would be coming home the next day, I didn't kiss her goodnight but left her sleeping while Bob sat with her.

She stopped breathing just before ten o'clock.

*   *   *

The minister gave her the funeral rally for eternal life. The church was packed with the friends and students she loved. The minister said she was still there with us, loving.

She had gone to find Pop, and her own immortality.

I was left with my version of immortality. Paper.

I only hope I can die with some of the dignity and faith of my mother.

Boys, you will never know your great-grandmother. But in a way you know her well—your own mom, Lily, who sang songs to you when you were in her womb and who has cared for you with a ceaseless passion ever since.

I TAKE LITERALLY THE STATEMENT IN THE GOS-
PEL OF JOHN THAT GOD LOVES THE WORLD.
I BELIEVE THAT THE WORLD WAS CREATED AND
APPROVED BY LOVE, THAT IT SUBSISTS, COHERES,
AND ENDURES BY LOVE, AND THAT, INSOFAR AS IT
IS REDEEMABLE, IT CAN BE REDEEMED ONLY BY
LOVE. I BELIEVE THAT DIVINE LOVE, INCARNATE
AND INDWELLING IN THE WORLD, SUMMONS THE
WORLD ALWAYS TOWARD WHOLENESS, WHICH IS
ULTIMATELY RECONCILIATION AND ATONEMENT
WITH GOD.

Wendell Berry

My shy Pop wanted to preach, to convert his fellow General Electric workers in the low-voltage switch gear department. But I doubt if any of them ever knew he called himself a Christian. Speaking up, even telling, left him petrified. When guests arrived at our house, Pop headed to his basement workshop to tinker with a project and didn't reappear until they had left. Social situations confounded him. Even consumed as he was by the love of Jesus, he left the speaking to Oral Roberts, & Billy Graham, sending them contributions and turning on the TV or radio only when one of them was preaching.

Once I asked Pop to tell me exactly what it was he believed. I wanted him to justify himself. His reply was, "If you don't know, I can't tell you," and he walked away. He could not tell. But in his quiet kindness he showed me.

BH/Journal

Dear Boys,

Since you are now in your teens you must wonder where these sex advice letters are tending. Well, of course, to The First Time. Oh happy day. . . .

Forget about that happy day stuff. What you are beginning is the start of a long pilgrimage interspersed with whoops of joy, utter agony, lots of cooing, devastating heartbreak and, I hope, in the end a long, deeply loving partnership with the person you are lucky enough to find in the maelstrom.

When you find that person never let go. Endure the waves of bliss and grief, laughter and anger. It's all worth it.

Here's how it happened for the teenage me . . . the first time (almost) and the first time for real.

Since the pretty, leaping cheerleaders figured I was too odd to notice, I gathered up nerve to ask Betty Howard, the class poet and artist, to the movies.

Betty talked nonstop and sneered at school spirit. I swore that if this date didn't work out I would give up on girls forever.

My first date with Betty was also the first time that Pop didn't have to chauffeur. I was sixteen and had my license. We went to a movie and then parked for hours in the Pontiac outside of the apartment house where she lived with her divorced father.

We talked about poetry and Jack Kerouac.

I decided I didn't care if she was fat and nothing to brag about back at school. Here was a girl who loved to read books and think deeply.

I invited her to my house the next day to read my journals. She read all of them, and I could see she was doing it with great care. She even commented in the margins: *Great!* or *Wow!* After my cynical "Sometimes it is necessary to be insincere," she wrote "Think again about this."

She gave me her paperback copy of Jack London's *Martin Eden,* with red underlinings of her favorite passages and *Tremendous soul!* or *What a poet!* in the margins.

The next Saturday, we went to another movie, and, afterward, we drove to Valley Forge. We parked under the Observation Tower and kissed, and she suggested that we climb to the top of the tower and experience Valley Forge's historical tradition in the moonlight, and write a poem.

We climbed over the locked gate with the warning about trespassing and walked the steps to the top. We hadn't started our poem, or even begun to experience the moonlit tradition yet, when a police cruiser pulled up down below and began poking around my car.

"Up here!" I called.

The cop picked us out with his spotlight.

"We're writing a poem!" I shouted down.

Driving home, Betty and I planned our great courtroom battles and composed our speeches about how poetry transcended petty trespassing laws and about how poets should be allowed to experience Valley Forge after hours. To us that cop was a symbol of the barbarian world out there. It was the two of us against the millions of them. Like Thoreau, we would go to jail before we'd give up our inmost beings to rules favoring property!

For weeks, we eagerly awaited our court summons. But it never came.

One night we drove to a distant town to hear Louis Armstrong. On the way, Betty told me all about jazz, who was good and who was great. When we got there, we stood at the edge of the dance floor, and shouted at Armstrong between numbers. "Hey, man, what you got in that cup?" Betty yelled up to the stage as Armstrong swigged from a tin cup.

"Just water, honey," the great man assured her.

Jazz, poetry, fiction, philosophy—Betty had them all under her belt. I could see there'd never be another girl that knew what Betty knew.

After the Armstrong concert, we walked to the car holding hands, and I reached in my pocket and took out the I Am His ring.

"I want you to have this," I said. "It doesn't mean anything shallow, like we are going steady or any of that. But I just want to give it to you."

She put her arm around my neck and said, "Ahh."

Inside the car, I ran my hand as far up her leg as she allowed.

I went to Ocean City for the summer. I didn't expect to see Betty again until the fall. But one day she telephoned me at the drugstore to say she had a mother's-helper job in Ocean City. The job was for a week, she said, and then she said *she would be alone in the house the first night.*

Could I come to see her when I got off work?

I said I'd be there—at midnight.

At midnight, we went for a walk on the beach, and thought about all the other thinkers who had paced the sands pondering the deeper meaning of life. Then we went back to the house. I telephoned Pop and said I was starting right back with the car. Betty got into her pajamas and kissed me good night.

That did it. She took off her pajama top, but stopped me when I tried to peel off her bottoms. We went to her bedroom and lay with my fingers hooked in her bottoms. We listened to the surf. If the church was right, this meant Hell. But I decided I'd risk it. I yanked on her bottoms again.

"Oh, okay," she sighed and stripped them off.

But that stopped it. After twelve hours at the store, I was tired. I wasn't getting anywhere except scared.

The phone rang. I looked at the clock. It was three A.M. We had been trying this for two hours and I had no excuses for Mom or Pop, and it was one or the other on the other end of the phone. So I didn't let Betty answer it.

I kissed her good night, very commandingly. I told her not to worry. It was a sin, I said, but maybe it was natural. I didn't know what I was talking about—what I wanted to do or what I couldn't do. I'd never heard the word impotence.

I was ten blocks from home when I saw a lone figure walking toward me—Mom. She was hiking the entire fifty-five blocks to get me.

I stopped the car and opened the door for her. She bit her lip and stared ahead. "Honest, Mom, nothing happened," I was able to say with some truth.

At home Pop pretended to be asleep. He said nothing the next day, either. In fact, he never did. But he must have complained to Mom plenty. He did that when he couldn't confront us.

Mom handed me a little booklet with two pages of information about sexual intercourse and twenty-two pages about syphilis and gonorrhea.

A month later Betty and I finished what we had started. But then she got hysterical and concocted a douche of Clorox. I got hysterical too. I thought I heard her father at the apartment door. So I kicked the screen from the window and readied myself for a three-story leap.

Every night afterward we consoled each other by phone. I promised Betty that when she had the baby we would go live at the seashore beneath the whispering pines. I promised we'd write poetry and read books forever.

But Betty didn't have a baby. She gained weight and began to babble and laugh in shouts. Then she dropped out of school and told me she tried to kill herself with an overdose of Bromo-Seltzer.

In my journal I wrote: "Betty is far from lost and has tremendous potential. I resolve never to give up on her improvement."

But what about Truth? Was this love play just frivolity? No. "Sex is natural and therefore part of truth," I wrote.

What's all this tell you boys? Not much. Your tale may be entirely different.

Betty went on to marry a good friend of mine, had four children with him, divorced, escaped to a cabin in northern New York. She lived and died in that cabin, surrounded by her pottery, her poetry and hundreds of books.

We were brave teenagers together on a long road. We were all we had in a vapid school and an incomprehensible universe.

"God" is a word that is odd to me. I like the Native American term "Great Spirit," for it is the Spirit of love and wonder that is huge in the human universe, the only universe I vaguely know. The other 95 percent is unknowable, I am told.

BH/Journal

Dear Boys,

Beware the opinions of experts, holy or secular.

From Descartes on, philosophy has often denigrated dogs and other animals. The result has been four hundred years of brutalization and laboratory vivisection without benefit of pain relief. Dogs, it seems, don't feel pain, and of course they don't have souls, as the church noted. So dogs have been fodder for our endless cruelty. Here's one of Descartes's disciples, Nicolas de Malebranche, with the master's doctrine on animals:

"There is neither intelligence nor souls as ordinarily meant. They eat without pleasure, cry without pain, grow without knowing it; they desire nothing, fear nothing, know nothing; and if they act in a manner that demonstrates intelligence, it is because God, having made them in order to preserve them, made their bodies in such a way that they mechanically avoid what is capable of destroying them."

In short, Descartes opined: I think therefore I am, you don't think therefore you aren't.

Any dog owner knows this is a crock. Theologians and philosophers cook up their crocks and hope for immortal tenure. Problem is they never get out of their crock kitchen.

Dear Boys,

I knew him as a silent, tired, older man. But there was more, there always is, and it still matters to you and me.

Just after he turned sixty, I had written to Pop from college: "I have lived all eighteen years of my life with you and I don't know anything about your past, your parents, your grandparents. Nothing. Please write back and tell me about your life."

No answer.

That summer Pop and I went fishing, the two of us alone in Ocean City's Great Egg Harbor Bay. With the rented rowboat anchored a mile from shore, he had no easy escape.

"Pop, I don't know anything about you," I began, dangling my feet in the water and holding the fishing pole for the fish that never bit that afternoon.

"There's nothing to know."

"Well, at least tell me where you grew up."

"In Audubon, New Jersey."

"What was it like?"

"We had a house near the Delaware."

"What else?"

"There was a lighted buoy on the river that I saw from my bedroom window. It flashed on and off every night. There isn't too much else. Once some kids broke a window in a neighbor's house and I got blamed."

"How long did you live in Audubon?"

"Just when I was young. Then my dad got a better job with Swift and Company and we moved to Philadelphia, to Fifty-second and Pine."

I waited, and fished.

"My brothers and I used to help dad load the Swift meat wagon at four in the morning and sometimes we'd go around with him and the company horse and I'd help him make deliveries to the butcher shops. He did a good job and they wanted to make him sales manager for all of South Jersey, but he didn't want it. He retired early."

"What kind of a guy was Grandpop then?"

Pop stopped and stared at the water. He pressed his lips together. "He drank."

Pop stopped and I waited.

"He used to crawl across the park at night on his hands and knees. Once my mother had to lock him in the closet for a day until he sobered up. Uncle Clarence and Uncle Jim grabbed him and dragged him upstairs and helped her shove him in the closet and she locked it. He begged to be let out but she wouldn't let him out."

Pop stared. "It was awful."

I didn't say anything.

"One day outside the house he came up the street drunk. I was with my mother and he grabbed her. I hit him."

"How?"

"Twice. In the stomach."

His lips worked but he didn't speak, trying to control his tears. "I ran away from home. I stayed with a neighbor around the block for two weeks. I didn't tell them where I was."

There was nothing more he wanted to say. He fished for the rest of the afternoon in silence. To Pop that had been everything, hitting his father.

Pop died suddenly in his sleep in 1968, when I was traveling in Rome. I wrote in my journal "Jesus took him gently home, that gentle man."

I thought we would have much more time to talk, It was not so.

Boys, talk to your father. There is always something important in him that you may not know. That goes for most everybody you meet.

ROME

On the morning
Pop said his prayers, slept
And died, I hiked
The Appian Way.
Once a chariot path, now
A miles long, gasoline fumed
Traffic jam.

For hours I slogged on
Towards the catacombs and
The remains of the
Cowering faithful
Paul wrote love letters to
Thousands of years ago.

A grumpy priest led me
Down into the hole
Where they had worshipped.
I saw skulls, bones,

Climbed into the Spring air
To find another love letter
At American Express.
"Call home urgent. Mom."

If you are a young pilgrim
In Rome and your father
Dies suddenly
You:
Laugh congratulations to him.
His Jesus took a gentle man
Gently.
"You did it Pop"!

You:
Try prayer, but
Forget how to or
Who to.

You:
Open the Word of God
In a Protestant church
But find too many words of God.

You:
Prowl ancient Catholic churches
With blank-eyed statues

Giggling school girls at confession
And bloody hanging corpses.

You:
Ask a priest to pray for Pop.
"And he was a Catholic, are you?"
You reach out to the priest,
Hold his arm,
Spanning the gap he just named.
"No."
"Of course I will pray for him."
He smiles tightly, sending you
and Pop to hell.

You:
Alone in a hotel room
With a pint of bourbon
For the first time
You cry.

I have always been amused and appalled by the preachers who announce they know exactly who God is. Kierkegaard described such theology as "an utter triviality" like trying to empty the ocean with a teaspoon and similar to an elephant passing gas.

BH/Journal

Virtual reality points to a boundless capacity for deception. Not simply by governments or corporations, but by hostile individuals acting on each other. We can do this today, but we are increasing the sophistication of deception faster than the technology of verification.

The consequence of that is the end of truth. The dark side of the information technology explosion is that it will breed a population that believes nothing and, perhaps even more dangerous, a population ready to believe only one "truth" fanatically and willing to kill for.

Alvin Toffler

Dear Boys,

For much of my late teen years and twenties booze was a serious problem for me. Later, the draft board wanted me to kill strangers in the Vietnam war. Cheap wine offered fake solutions to a persistent loneliness and threats of the draft board. Awful times that are too painful to document here. For a few sober years I was married to Nancy, an ex-nun, but when that ended I almost hit bottom. If I had I would have joined Alcoholic Anonymous, and I suggest AA to you if you ever need it, as a way back.

AA's *Big Book,* published in 1939, has sold millions of copies. In it, AA founder Bill W., a rum-ruined God-mocker, describes how an old friend who had "got religion" convinced him to try self-abnegation.

"I humbly offered myself to God, as I then understood Him, to do with me as He would. I placed myself unreservedly under His care and direction. I admitted for the first time that of myself I was nothing; that without Him I was lost. . . .

"Common sense would thus become uncommon sense. I was to sit quietly when in doubt, asking only for direction and strength to meet my problems as

He would have me. Never was I to pray for myself, except as my requests bore on my usefulness to others. Then only might I expect to receive. But that would be in great measure. . . .

"Simple, but not easy: a price had to be paid. It meant destruction of self-centeredness. I must turn in all things to the Father of Light who presides over us all.

"These were revolutionary and drastic proposals, but the moment I fully accepted them, the effect was electric. There was a sense of victory, followed by such peace and serenity as I had never known. There was utter confidence. I felt lifted up, as though the great clean wind of a mountain top blew through and through. God comes to most men gradually, but His impact on me was sudden and profound."

"FAITH IS WHAT SOMEONE KNOWS TO BE TRUE,
WHETHER THEY BELIEVE IT OR NOT."
Flannery O'Connor

FOR THE FIRST TIME IN 4 BILLION YEARS A LIVING CREATURE HAD CONTEMPLATED HIMSELF AND HEARD WITH A SUDDEN, UNACCOUNTABLE LONELINESS, THE WHISPER OF WIND IN THE NIGHT REEDS.

Loren Eiseley, on the dawn of consciousness

Dear Boys,

Here's an incident that may mean a bit to you in the future. Certainly my humiliation was nothing compared to the protests of civil right champions soon to come in the '60's.

But I was amazed by the vicious reaction of the sophomore goons in charge of guarding school tradition.

Hamilton College was a men's school in farm country, on top of a hill, miles from the nearest city. I intended to live like a monk on that hill, searching for God.

Only beanies brought me to action. When the sophomores enforced the wearing of beanies by freshmen during the first semester, I aimed a loudspeaker at the quad through a dormitory window. "Freshmen, burn your beanies! If you give in to the sophomore tyrants, you will give in to the Communists too!"

For many nights I yelled that from the window. But I made sure it was somebody else's room.

Later, in an attempt to be reasonable and direct, I went to the head of the sophomore honor society, who was responsible for directing the beanie-wearing tradition. I told him how the beanies resembled the stars imposed on Jews by Nazis.

He smiled and thanked me for the visit.

The next week, after compulsory Tuesday chapel, I was grabbed from behind by the four goons and hustled down the chapel steps, my books scattering behind me. While eight hundred men jeered and the dean smiled indulgently, I was crowned with a baby bonnet and had to wear a sign around my neck. "Baby" it said. I was betrayed, crucified and honored.

A few years later the college banned beanies.

Boys, do not be surprised if any new idea you come up with results in a similar response.

*   *   *

A few years later I found myself at the center of international passions I never saw coming. Remember when you raise your hand in protest, you may not be alone.

The Lead Pencil Club was founded in the middle of a December night in 1993 when I discovered some Luddite sentiments in my friend Doris Grumbach's memoir *Extra Innings*. She was sick of her word processor and other gadgets and wished they would catch a virus for which there was no cure. "Why not use a lead pencil?," I asked myself. "Why not a lead pencil club, for those of us who agree with her?" The next day I called Doris with my idea and she liked it. I discovered that Henry David Thoreau was the son of a pencil maker and helped his father manufacture pencils. Indeed, it is quite probable that *Walden* was written with a pencil that Thoreau made himself. He became a Founder emeritus of our new club with his father, John Thoreau, as proprietor. Our Club was conceived in the spirit of amazed outrage tinged with humor. Our Manifesto, was mentioned in a local newspaper after I mailed it to the editor, expecting to be ignored. Instead, it appeared, and I was deluged with mail in response. I next wrote to *The New York Times* Op Ed page expecting nothing and was instead featured. The Manifesto and news of our club appeared in the Paris-based *International Herald Tribune, Time, Newsweek, The L.A. Times Book Review, Newsday,* and news services around the world. A German magazine, *Spotlight,* fashioned a one-on-one debate between Bill Gates and this writer. From all areas of the earth, letters arrived in pencil. Our correspondents wrote that they were baffled, infuriated and personally and financially injured by the onslaught of the all-pervasive electronic snake oil in their homes, offices, libraries, and schools. To them the lead pencil became a symbol of defiance at the digital colonization of this planet, just as Gandhi's spinning wheel symbolized the resistance of the people of India faced with England's imperialism. To our members it seems we are destined to be born in electronics, bathed in it all our lives and ushered out like chickens in a barn that never see the real light of day.

What is now at stake for you guys is not just the oppression of omnipresent machines, it is our entire vision of what people are for. In that I was instructed by our members and to them I am thankful.

Dear Boys,

With puberty comes an increasing awareness of death and life thereafter. Perhaps it might be best to think of eternal life as what it is not; not a *New York Times* obituary, not a book selected for the canon of English literature; not a boulevard named for you. Eternal life, as I understand "The Prayer of St. Francis," is the enduring soul of all humanity. We experience that soul by surrendering the cobbled-together construct of ourselves to each other, to those living and to those to come and who came before us. The ego is a fraud.

Beyond that limited understanding I cannot reach. St. Francis saw what I can't see. But I trust him. I recognize his vision of immortality as true. And so did many others.

Dostoevsky: "If you were to destroy in mankind the belief in immortality, not only love but every living force maintaining the life of the world would at once be dried up."

Spinoza: "We feel and know that we are eternal."

Rousseau: "Not all the subtleties of metaphysics can make me doubt a moment of the immortality of the soul, and of a beneficent providence. I feel it, I believe it, I desire it, I hope it, and will defend it to my last breath."

Bored? Nothing to do? Consider this: 30,000 children die every day worldwide. Maybe you should be doing something.

BH/Journal

Dear Boys,

As a college sophomore, I was so lost that I attached myself to an older fellow who seemed to have all the answers. Turns out he didn't. He was as lost as I was. But I found three words that became my own answers.

In my sophomore year I joined a wolf pack, fellows, usually drunk, who risked their lives to drive hours down the icy thruway to the nearest girls' schools. We swaggered into the dorms of Vassar with real fear and hate, brushing unattractive "ughmoes" aside, looking for beauty and love.

The leader of the pack was Woodward Flagler, a tall, skinny, pimple-faced kid who had discovered Paul Goodman, author of *Growing up Absurd*. He had invited him to spend a weekend on campus teaching, and had actually raised the money to pay him. When one of Flagler's professors expressed reservations about Goodman's ideas in a panel debate, Flagler boycotted the professor's class for the rest of the semester and still got an A. The faculty treated Flagler not as a student, not as an equal, but as a superior. To me, and others, he was a god, a new father.

Woody announced to us that he was a Renaissance man. We didn't know what that was. But Woody, reclining in his throne—a plastic lawn chair, the only furniture in his room—said he intended to be an authority on everything, beginning with the jazz that his stereo blared, to movies and art and philosophy and technology and nuclear physics. The universe was Woody's, just as it had been Pop's through his God. I was seeing an authority I'd seen before.

When Woody paraded into the lounges of girls' school dorms at the head of the pack, unshaved, his red hair uncombed, wearing his black basketball sneakers, and more than once sporting the tops of his pajamas, he created instant theater. Women who were at first amused or made nervous by Woody's zaniness were quickly bullied by the zealotry in his glaring eyes and his demanding voice.

Woody would instruct on any topic and often quoted Goodman: "Grace, Love, Community." He also let his pack know which women were beautiful and which were to be ignored. He understood beauty in women and art. I didn't. I obeyed.

Woody's power was not confined to campus.

He and I took a government class field-trip to Washington. On our tour Woody brought along his ever-present bag of popcorn. He would down several bags of popcorn a day and unceremoniously regurgitate as much as he could of it—an act of defiance and bravado. He did just this on the White House lawn.

He swaggered through visits to Gerry Ford, a leader of the House of Representatives at the time, and with Jimmy Hoffa, head of the powerful Teamsters Union. Woody took over the conversation from the stammering government professor who was our tour tutor, and conducted the discussions with Ford and Hoffa on his own terms. He was most impressed with Hoffa, who said power was everything, and either you had it or you didn't, big people and little people. Woody said, yeah, that was the way the world worked.

I didn't dare ask him what Goodman would say. I didn't want to lose Woody's friendship by seeming critical. He was touchy and quick to rage.

One night Woody took on an entire theater watching the movie *Tea and Sympathy*. "This is sentimental bullshit!" he hooted and threw popcorn at the screen. I dragged him from the theater when a burly fellow threatened to get tough. Woody unsuccessfully tried to break a Coke bottle to fight him with.

We were boarding at the home of a Representative from Ulster County, New York. That night

Woody collared the Representative and informed him that his political future in the county was quits, unless he listened up to Woody Flagler, who had been a summer reporter for a Kingston newspaper. I noticed that the Representative listened to Woody for half an hour, asking questions and soliciting advice.

In campus politics Woody was rising fast, even among those who despised him for his slovenliness and his belching and farting. Woody was elected to two terms as fraternity president, demanded and won from the dean the right of agnostics to avoid compulsory chapel, and organized with Mark Marshall, one of three campus blacks, the picketing of a hotel chain for their racial discrimination. His and Mark's demonstration made national headlines, was featured on all three network TV news programs, and helped start all the civil-rights demonstrations and student uprisings from 1961 on.

For art class I attempted a self-portrait in oil paint. I had always wanted to look like a thoughtful person. In my high-school yearbook I had posed gazing into the distance mystically, much as I imagined Thoreau did. The effect was a glassy-eyed stare suggestive of narcotic stupor. Now, for my art class self-portrait I paid particular attention to the eyes—

glaring, no nonsense. I hung the finished portrait on my wall, thinking it was a fine idea of what I was all about.

The only trouble was, I could never convince anyone it was a picture of me and not Woody.

Then, in a Saturday night wolf-pack raid on Vassar, Woody and I found ourselves pursuing the same blonde. She preferred me. On the drive back, Flagler screamed that I was a Judas and no longer his friend.

For a month he talked around me, stared through me and refused to acknowledge I existed, which in a way, since I had become him, I didn't mind.

That winter, in one of the final journal entries, I wrote: "I have no ideas and no reason for anything. I am nothing. I couldn't even complain if somebody wanted to kill me." Or why not step out in front of a truck?

I announced I was leaving school. I'd go south, where it was warm, and I'd write. Nobody cared. As I was waiting for a midnight cab, Mark Marshall came to my room.

As one of the few campus Black students, he understood something of rejection. "Don't go. I'll miss you," he said quietly. That scrap of affection was all I needed.

"But how do I think?" I begged.

He mentioned Occam's Razor. "Shave away the nonessentials and you'll find the real." I complained that I had already done that and I had found nothing.

On a day soon after Mark's visit, Flagler was in the room. Somebody asked Flagler, "Do you think war is always wrong?"

"That depends if you think life is sacred or not," Woody threw out. (The small moment that changed so much as I discussed earlier.)

To Pop, not only war, but any harm—even to a tree branch—was wrong.

To Pop, life *was* sacred. Sure, he never said that but he must have thought that, or felt it.

I heard Flagler's words as if they were Pop's. "Life is sacred," I heard as my silent father's motto of mottoes.

Besides, what was the value of trying to figure out life if you didn't honor life itself? I concluded.

With my new first premise, I treated others with reverence. But then I was to be revered too. Pop could have said that. Over the years a voice emerged that I came to recognize as my own.

Closing out the journal I wrote: "Flippancy to any living thing, even an ear of corn, is wrong.

Every action is moral. Every action must be excellent."

It wasn't *the* Truth from *the* God, but it was a truth I remembered from long ago, and it would do.

Pop had left me his gentleness, his caring, the possibility of something sacred.

This was all I needed to know about my hidden father. Life is indeed sacred.

And probably all we will ever need to know about anything.

All human nature vigorously resists grace because grace changes us and the change is painful.
Flannery O'Connor

Dear Boys,

Here is William Faulkner's Nobel Prize acceptance speech, 1950. In part, he addresses it to you.

"I feel that this award was not made to me as a man, but to my work—a life's work in the agony and sweat of the human spirit, not for glory and least of all for profit, but to create out of the materials of the human spirit something which did not exist before. So this award is only mine in trust. It will not be difficult to find a dedication for the money part of it commensurate with the purpose and significance of its origin. But I would like to do the same with the acclaim too, by using this moment as a pinnacle from which I might be listened to by the young men and women already dedicated to the same anguish and travail, among whom is already that one who will someday stand here where I am standing.

"Our tragedy today is a general and universal physical fear so long sustained by now that we can even bear it. There are no longer problems of the spirit. There is only the question: When will I be blown up? Because of this, the young man or woman writing today has forgotten the problems of the human heart in conflict with itself which alone can make good writing because only that is worth writing about, worth the agony and the sweat.

"He must learn them again. He must teach himself that the basest of all things is to be afraid; and, teaching himself that, forget it forever, leaving no room in his workshop for anything but the old verities and truths of the heart, the old universal truths lacking which any story is ephemeral and doomed—love and honor and pity and pride and compassion and sacrifice. Until he does so, he labors under a curse. He writes not of love but of lust, of defeats in which nobody loses anything of value, of victories without hope and, worst of all, without pity or compassion. His griefs grieve on no universal bones, leaving no scars. He writes not of the heart but of the glands.

"Until he relearns these things, he will write as though he stood among and watched the end of man. I decline to accept the end of man. It is easy enough to say that man is immortal simply because he will endure: that when the last ding-dong of doom has clanged and faded from the last worthless rock hanging tideless in the last red and dying evening, that even then there will still be one more sound: that of his puny inexhaustible voice, still talking. I refuse to accept this. I believe that man will not merely endure: he will prevail. He is immortal, not because he alone among creatures has an inexhaustible voice, but because he has a soul, a spirit capable of compassion and sacrifice and endurance. The poet's, the writer's, duty is to write about these things. It is his privilege to help man endure by lifting his heart, by reminding him of the courage and honor and hope and pride and compassion and pity and sacrifice which have been the glory of his past. The poet's voice need not merely be the record of man, it can be one of the props, the pillars to help him endure and prevail."

Chartres Cathedral's beauty is not achieved because its designers considered themselves to be builders of perfection. In fact, part of the impact of Chartres is its very imperfection. The unequal spires, the slanting floor, the slightly off center Royal Portal and countless other mistakes that only prove that human beings—sinners, if you will—fashioned this building, often without complete plans and by the seat of their pants.

BH/Journal

I believed in you, my Soul . . .

Loaf with me on the grass, loose the stop from your throat . . .

Only the lull I like, the hum of your valved voice.

I mind how once we lay, such a transparent summer morning.

Swiftly across and spread around me the peace and knowledge that pass all the argument of the earth,

And I know that the hand of God is the promise of my own,

And I know that the spirit of God is the brother of my own,

And that all the men ever born are also my brothers and the women my sisters and lovers,

And that a kelson of the creation is love.

Watt Whitman

Dear Boys,

Some day you guys may think about starting your own business. The conventional cliche is that you need big time start-up capital.

Not so. Sometimes lots of money gets in the way of a vision. Here's how the Pushcart Press started. Your story may be different, but remember it is the dream that counts, not the cash.*

"Mills Hotel for Men, Number 2" was engraved in stone over the entrance to the Bleecker Street building where I lived in 1977. Theodore Dreiser once lived there too, but, until a recent remodeling, the Mills Hotel had been a flophouse. A few years earlier a resident wino had pitched a table out a high window and killed a pedestrian. It made the papers.

My sixth-floor studio apartment faced west. Between buildings I could glimpse the smokestacks of ships on the Hudson River, but not the river itself. In an unshaded window across the street two naked guys under a light bulb adored each other's bodies and invited neighbors to adore them. In the apart-

* See *The Publish if Yourself Handbook* (various editions) 1973–1987 for details.

ment under me a woman wailed orgasmically every morning, but I never heard another voice in her room. Tourists crowded the streets below, seeking a whiff of New York fifties bohemia, but only a few coffeehouses with faded photos of Beat greats remained from those days.

I was a would-be publisher, recently fired from Doubleday, with four titles on my list: the universally rejected, self-published novel I had consumed eight years in writing; a popular handbook that told other writers how to publish their own work, and the first two editions of my annual *Pushcart Prize* anthology of poetry, essays, and stories from little magazines and small presses, assembled now for 50 years with the help of hundreds of contributors.

Pushcart Press, I had named myself. The press occupied the space under the double bed. The bed filled most of the apartment and was supported by boxes of books. In good weeks, the bed sank closer to the floor as orders left, carried on my back in number one mailbags to the nearby Prince Street post office. In bad weeks, when unsold books were returned, the bed rose again, sometimes at an awkward angle.

I was poor, but honorable in my poverty. Once, at lunch with Harvey Shapiro, editor of *The New York*

Times Book Review, I complained that I wouldn't mind publishing at least one bestseller.

"You couldn't," he snapped, disappointed that I had even thought of lowering myself to a bestseller.

Boys, if you want to be noble, don't expect to be rich too. Later on Pushcart did rather well, winning awards from Publishers Weekly, The National Book Critics Circle, Poets & Writers, and The American Academy of Arts & Letters.

But riches, ruinous riches never!

PLENTY DESTROYS A NATION AND A PERSON.
John Steinbeck

The cyberspace cadets have concocted a new religion complete with a passel of techno-evangelists and their own special priestly lingo. According to them, the computer is the most stunning advance since the capture of fire. They preach that soon nothing will be the same. Their gospel rejoices that we are witnessing the end of the human race. Soon we may be replaced by an electronic superbeing. Forward we all rush, toward we know not what.

BH / Journal / 1995

WHAT AN ASTONISHING THING A BOOK IS. IT'S A FLAT OBJECT MADE FROM A TREE WITH FLEXIBLE PARTS ON WHICH ARE IMPRINTED LOTS OF FUNNY DARK SQUIGGLES. BUT ONE GLANCE AT IT AND YOU'RE INSIDE THE MIND OF ANOTHER PERSON, MAYBE SOMEBODY DEAD FOR THOUSANDS OF YEARS. ACROSS THE MILLENNIA, AN AUTHOR IS SPEAKING CLEARLY AND SILENTLY INSIDE YOUR HEAD, DIRECTLY TO YOU. WRITING IS PERHAPS THE GREATEST OF HUMAN INVENTIONS, BINDING TOGETHER PEOPLE WHO NEVER KNEW EACH OTHER, CITIZENS OF DISTANT EPOCHS. BOOKS BREAK THE SHACKLES OF TIME. A BOOK IS PROOF THAT HUMANS ARE CAPABLE OF WORKING MAGIC.

Carl Sagan

Rev. Dr. Martin Luther King, Jr. on Love

"Probably no admonition of Jesus has been more difficult to follow than the command to "love your enemies." Some people have sincerely felt that its actual practice is not possible. It is easy, they say, to love those who love you, but how can one love those who openly and insidiously seek to defeat you? . . . This command of Jesus challenges us with new urgency. Upheaval after upheaval has reminded us that modern humanity is traveling along a road called hate, in a journey that will bring us to destruction. . . . Far from being the pious injunction of a Utopian dreamer, the command to love one's enemy is an absolute necessity for our survival. Love even for enemies is the key to the solution of the problems of our world. Jesus is not an impractical idealist: he is the practical realist.

"I am certain that Jesus understood the difficulty inherent in the act of loving one's enemy. He never joined the ranks of those who talk glibly about the easiness of the moral life. He realized that every genuine expression of love grows out of a consistent and total surrender to God. So when Jesus said 'Love your

enemy,' he was not unmindful of its stringent quali-
ties. Yet he meant every word of it. Our responsibil-
ity as Christians is to discover the meaning of this
command and seek passionately to live it out in our
daily lives. . . .

"When Jesus bids us to love our enemies, he is
speaking of neither *eros* [romantic love] nor *philia*
[reciprocal love of friends]; he is speaking of *agape,*
understanding and creative, redemptive goodwill for
all people. Only by following this way and respond-
ing with this type of love are we able to be children
of our Father who is in Heaven."

Dear Boys,

May I make a suggestion that you make music a center of your life? I say this as a word guy, an author and a publisher. Words can only take us so far. We need music to continue our reach.

When I was a kid music didn't happen at home. My Pop sometimes dutifully played hymns on the piano, now and then, and in school we were taught instruments (mine was the trumpet) by dull teachers that long ago had lost all fervor for music. All they taught us was attention to notes.

In church we often sang hymns without any passion for words or music. The same old same old Sunday after Sunday. But not always.

When I joined the little church down the road from our East Hampton house, it was a hymn, "Be Thou my Vision," that brought me back to the possibilities of religion. "This is who I am!" I exulted in my journal.

Here are music memories that might be helpful to you.

In school it was thought by education pundits that music inoculated kids against juvenile delinquency and made them appreciate the finer things. Music was practical. Plus, said the guidance counselor, trumpet-playing would look good on my permanent record. I would appear "well-rounded" for college admissions (well-rounded was a top virtue of the times). Music was a higher-education insurance policy.

I practiced mightily and progressed to first rank in the junior and senior high school brass sections. In eleventh grade, when I was named drum major of the Lower Merion High School marching band, I strode onto the halftime football field and blasted my whistle at the musicians under my glorious command. We attempted to entertain the uninterested crowd with our squawking of "Semper Fidelis," "The Thunderer," or "Stars and Stripes Forever." Then we fled the field in ragged lines blaring the school fight song.

I was becoming very well-rounded.

* * *

With my brother and a few friends I started a dance band—the Continentals. Like thousands of boys then and since, we thought music was the key to fame, fortune, and girls. I figured we'd become as famous as the Paul Whiteman band, a big deal at the time. But Saturday practice sessions often ended quickly as we took up our real interest—driveway basketball.

We Continentals managed to learn only two songs—"Beat Me Daddy Eight to the Bar" and "You Always Hurt the One You Love." Our first gig was a Methodist teen dance. Our two selections lasted only a few minutes. We knew no other tunes. That was it for the Continentals. The minister scrambled around for a record player to fill the void.

Our washed-out school music teachers had long ago lost any zeal for their profession. Years of listening to students butcher the classics had worn them down. They never hinted to me, or they had forgotten entirely, how music could revolutionize heart and soul. However, I was told that a knowledge of classical music was important for college.

I borrowed Beethoven's Fifth Symphony from the library. It was one of the few symphonies I had heard of. I lay on the couch, determined to listen carefully and find out what use this music would be to me. At one point, the theme seems to dissolve as if Beethoven is done with it. Then, as any Beethoven lover knows in the gut, it begins again almost imperceptibly and gathers to a roar of affirmation. Here, I was propelled to my feet in ecstasy. So that's what music can be, I suddenly knew.

*   *   *

Ever since joining our little neighborhood church I treasure some of the grand old hymns. My great joy is to sing them with people like me who hold them deep in their memories and call them forth with passion.

In summer at the nondenominational Rockbound Chapel, fastened to a granite boulder on a hill over the sea in Brooklin, Maine, I sing songs with other summer visitors—strangers and people I barely know. In untrained, inelegant, often too-loud or too-soft voices, we sing to each other of our pain, loneliness, and fear, topics we would hesitate to admit flat out in gatherings after services. We also sing of love, grace, trust, hope, peace—sentiments that are left out of the usual daily patter. We sing words that matter to us.

We are a mixed lot in age, sex, and occupation. We are fishermen, poets, CEOs, clerks, teachers, publishers, builders, mechanics, retirees, holiday rusticators, and others. We sing out our souls for each other. Our hymns are like hugs.

We are Protestants, Catholics, and those who would prefer not to be labeled. Some of us are of troubled faith and others are more agnostic than not. Even if our pew companions don't exactly share creeds, our hymns carry all of us to those Thin Places described by the Irish, elevated states of consciousness where almost all barriers between mortals and gods vanish.

Most of us Rockbound singers, like everybody else, spend portions of our days listening to music on our radios, TVs, or other devices. We are sung at. But in the tiny chapel we find our own voices. It makes no difference how well we sing, only that we do so. We raise our notes to each other and to heaven. No celebrity musician ever receives as much fan-love as we humble amateurs do, from each other, from the spirit within and around us.

Words, mere words, flat on the page or preached dead in the air, can ruin faith and often divide congregations. Theological niceties spun by divine theorists for centuries have led to ridiculous and murderous quarrels. Are we saved by grace or works? Does God recognize full-body baptism or a sprinkle? On and on the words of dogma spin into an eternity of nonsense.

A great preacher can almost lift mere words into the realm of song, but some don't even come close. Their verbiage leaves me annoyed, bored, betrayed, or asleep. During some sermons in various churches,

I daydream that I had brought a basket of ripe fruit to lob at the pulpit. Why should I sit here politely listening? I think, gazing out the window at the blowing tree limbs, the rushing clouds, or the tombstones of the blessedly dead.

We forget such sermons as quickly as possible. We also may forget even the words of wonderful sermons. But hymns—the classic, lasting hymns—resonate from childhood on. Even those of us who haven't warmed a pew in decades can recall hymns we learned in Sunday School, and in such songs our childhood faith is often restored.

William James observes in *The Varieties of Religious Experience* (1902): "In mystical literature such self-contradictory phrases as 'dazzling obscurity' 'whispering silence' and 'teeming desert' are continuously met with. They prove that not conceptual speech, but music rather is the element through which we are best spoken to by mystical truth."

Music is transcendent theology. Hildegard of Bingen, the twelfth-century mystic and composer, took music so seriously that in one of her plays, while the soul and the angels sing, the devil has only a speaking part. Music has been denied him. Because of his unmelodic nature, he can't approach the Thin Places.

Of course, not all hymns take us there. In fact, some common songs propel us in the opposite direction. They leave us lip-syncing the verses, deflated by trivial or sappy tunes and lyrics, Muzak for the well-fed, somnolent mind. For me, a mediocre hymn is as bad as a lousy sermon, because I am expected to participate in the debacle by at least pretending to sing along.

But oh! When it hits! When a great hymn reaches way down inside where you live: then the problem is not shall I sing, but can I manage to sing at all. I choke up and stumble over words and notes.

Such hymns go to a source in us beyond our control and leave us overwhelmed with joy and recognition. Suddenly, when words and music combine, I see, as in the tremendous line of "Amazing Grace"— "I was blind but now I see." On paper that line may not mean much. In song, it's almost more truth than I can bear to express.

Music may literally lift you out of your seats.

EVERY DOGMA HAS ITS DAY, BUT GOOD MUSIC
LIVES FOREVER.
Vernon Duke

"UP THE FUNNEL OF THE STAIRCASE CAME WARM WHIFFS OF JOINTS ROASTING, OF FOWLS BASTING, OF SOUPS SIMMERING—RAVISHING ALMOST AS FOOD ITSELF . . . MIXING WITH THE SMELL OF FOOD WERE FURTHER SMELLS—SMELLS OF CEDARWOOD AND SANDAL WOOD AND MAHOGANY; SCENTS OF MALE BODIES AND FEMALE BODIES; OF MEN SERVANTS AND MAID SERVANTS; OF COATS AND TROUSERS; OF CRINOLINES AND MANTLES; OF CURTAINS OF TAPESTRY, OF CURTAINS OF PLUSH; OF COAL DUST AND FOG; OF WINE AND CIGARS. EACH ROOM AS HE PASSED IT—DINING-ROOM, DRAWING-ROOM, LIBRARY, BEDROOM—WAFTED OUT ITS OWN CONTRIBUTION TO THE GENERAL STEW."

Virginia Woolf in *Flush*
Boys, Never think you know more
than your dog.

Dear Boys,

Sometime you make a fool of yourself and you are forgiven. In fact, your entire life is about to be changed.

Deep in my cups on February 22, 1978 at a fancy New York party, I was chatting up comedian Woody Allen at the bar when exploding flash bulbs announced the entry of Lauren Bacall, the actress. Right behind her was another actress, Ellen Burstyn I thought.

But it was really Genie, your future grandmom.

Somebody tapped me on the shoulder, and introduced me to "Ellen Burstyn," but I quickly forgot Genie's name in all the hubub. Nearby was Walter Cronkite, the CBS Evening News announcer and a national icon of news. Years ago he had witnessed Neil Armstrong step down from the moon lander and say, "That's one small step for (a) man, a giant leap for mankind."

I plowed through the room, spilling my white wine and hugged Walter gently. "I want you to know, Walter, that when you cried about the moon landing, I cried too. I loved you for your tears. You are no fake!"

There. I'd said it.

I spun off into the dark hall.

The place was jammed with gods. Gods of this, gods of that.

Authors Wilfrid Sheed and John Updike sat at a table talking. I flopped down at one end of the table, waved at Wilfrid, whom I had met once, and wondered about all of this.

"These are my people," I concluded to myself. "I belong here. We have all come through. We stuck to it. We did not subside into mediocrity."

I remember a big dim room, with dozens of round tables, and a small rostrum with a reading light at the head table. There was food of some sort, and there were speeches, by literary icons William Styron and then Ralph Ellison, who would not stop talking.

I tiptoed to the bar just outside the room and stood alone waiting for Ellison to finish.

Then "Ellen Burstyn" was again beside me.

I kissed her cheek.

Our very first kiss. (Almost 45 years ago.)

Somebody hushed us. We were talking too loudly, and had become a boozy spectacle.

I exited to the Men's Room and when I returned "Ellen" Genie had disappeared. I set off in search of her, spilling my wine in haste, but the 69th Street Armory is vast, a block long on each side.

I was about to go when I saw another woman suddenly left alone. It was Ruth Carter Stapleton, evangelist and healer from Plains, Georgia. And sister of the president of the United States, Jimmy Carter.

Why was she sitting by herself ignored? Didn't this snooty crowd approve of President Carter? He who had kissed Russian leader Brezhnev? A Christian kiss for an enemy. That would have been a big hoo-haa with this bunch.

And they probably didn't approve of Ruth, either. She had written a book about her beer-swilling, gas-pumping brother, Billy. Too unliterary for this lot?

Not for me.

As with Walter, I had essential information to convey to Ruth.

I placed my glass on the coffee table in front of her and sat down hard. "Hi! I'm Bill Henderson."

"Ruth Stapleton," she said.

"I know. I know who you are. You're the only evangelist I've ever seen for real in person since Billy Graham. Ocean City, New Jersey, about 1948. He was in a big circus tent by the boardwalk and you could hear the ocean breaking outside the tent. My dad took me there. He was very religious, believed in faith healing. This was a really big moment. Billy Graham was new in town. New everywhere, for that matter. And my dad and I sat on wooden folding chairs in the back of the tent and my dad let me sit on the aisle side so I could see straight up the aisle to the microphone where Billy spoke."

I stopped for a breath in my rambles.

"Yes?" she smiled, encouraging me.

"You want to hear more?"

I stared into her eyes, unsure.

"Certainly."

"My dad was one of the few guys I ever met anywhere who really believed. I mean really, really believed. No doubts. He talked to Jesus all the time. Even on the job. The world around him hardly even existed."

A crowd was pushing out of the dining area. Some of the diners came our way.

I found I was holding Ruth's hand.

I didn't care what the others thought.

She tightened her grip on my hand, so that I wouldn't pull away. "Tell me more about you and your dad."

"It seemed like we were the good guys, my dad and I and Billy Graham and everybody in the tent. I'd heard of the Communists and I was only seven years old so I didn't know what all that was, except it was evil. And we were good, and if I looked up I might see Jesus and His angels riding like cowboys across the clouds. Our guys!" I hooted.

I held her hand tighter.

"All those summers in Ocean City my mom and dad took us to church twice on Sunday, morning and evening, and outside the windows of the chapel I'd see the sinners dragging their rafts to and from the beach when they should have been in church with us. We would have to fix that. I sang with my dad and mom so those sinners could hear us and be saved. All summer long we sang."

I gazed into Ruth's eyes. Again I began to sing: "Trust and obey, for there's no other way . . ."

She knew the words. She joined me.

In the middle of that humming, laughing, drinking, clever mob, we squeezed each other's hands and we sang: "Trust and obey, for there's no other way, to be happy in Jesus, but to trust and obey."

When we finished the last verse in our solitude, I was tearing up. I had no more words left. I bent over and kissed her on the lips.

And she kissed me back.

Then I knew I was terribly, dangerously drunk and had to get out of there without crashing head-first onto the table in front of us.

"'Bye," I managed, and lurched up, holding onto the couch arm and her hand. She steadied me.

I realized that I must not open my mouth again. I had said all that I was permitted to say at this party.

I loped through the celebrities, hoping to spot my Ellen Burstyn. But she was nowhere.

So I left, stumbling down the Armory's stone stairs onto Park Avenue.

In that cold February night, three words began to rearrange themselves in my brain. "If Ruth's God is Love; then Love is God."

That's simple. Who could deny that Love is God?

Sure you could deny it in reverse. You could say to Ruth there is no God. Therefore God is not Love.

Or there are horrors in the universe. Therefore, God is not Love. But love? Love does not make earthquakes, bombs, holocausts. Love is God. That works.

Wordplay. I played with the words.

"Find me one person who would deny that love is everything for everybody," I said, looking up and down the empty sidewalk.

And what is sin?

Sin is the withholding of love from another person. From yourself, too. That's what sin is.

And since we all do this to each other and to ourselves all the time—withhold love—we are all sinners.

"Sin is failing to love!" I shouted, startled at this revelation.

On that early morning street, thirty years after Pop took me to see Billy Graham in his tent, I finally understood something about God, Love, and Sin. About Jesus.

Then I was simply amazed.

"I just kissed the sister of the president of the United States on the lips!" I whispered to myself.

"And she kissed me back!"

* * *

Days later by questioning friends of friends of friends, Genie tracked me down in a city of eight million people. On March 2, 1978, we had a drink at the Lion's Head pub in Greenwich Village.

The boozing boy found forgiveness. And Genie and I set off on the pilgrimage that led to Lily's birth on March 14, 1984 and you two on February 27, 2018.

I call this Grace. You will find Grace constantly in your lives. Don't hunt for Grace. It will find you when you least expect it.

After Pop's funeral, the crocuses were up and the willow leaves were starting. Mom and I talked in the back yard.

"I'm surprised there wasn't at least some joy for Pop's going to heaven," I said. "You all say you are Christians and we will see each other again, but nobody mentioned that."

She nodded. "Daddy's in heaven. I think of all the beautiful sights he's seeing now—even more beautiful than these flowers. But I'm alone and that's why I'm sad. I have to live on earth and fill out the tax forms and take care of the car, and do all the things by myself that we used to do together. Daddy's happy. I shouldn't be sad. I guess I'm just selfish."

BH/Journal

Dear Boys,

As I collect this book you two are five years old. You adore Grandmother Genie, rush to her hugs with joy. And she in turn lives each day with love for you.

But Genie and I are entering our 80's. Who knows how long we have to see you grow up and know you as teens and beyond, and you to know us. Perhaps Genie and I will be the grandparents known only in photographs.

So to keep Genie for you here is a synopsis of who she was and is.

A doctor's daughter, Genie grew up traveling about the country, from her birth in Birmingham Alabama, to stints in Seattle to New Orleans to Lexington, Kentucky. But her happiest memories are of summers with her storytelling grandmother in Corinth, Mississippi.

Genie was and is a dreamer.

After she graduated first in her acting class at Northwestern University, she headed to New York with most of the rest of her group, because that's where all actors scrambled for jobs and careers.

But Genie was not a careerist. Turning up for auditions seemed like work. Instead she dreamed up adventures—like Supergirls, a woman-funded, woman-staffed business that helped people with projects and problems. Genie loved to help, still does, which is why we and others love her.

Soon after she dreamed up Supergirls she sat down at dinner next to Howard Smith, a *Village Voice* columnist. He asked her what she did and she told him about Supergirls. He mentioned her dream in his next column.

In the months ahead, business picked up. *Look* magazine wanted to do a feature. When Genie explained they had no office, and only a few clients, *Look* said they'd produce the whole layout with a borrowed office and friends as clients. A three-page spread.

Johnny Carson's show called, the popular tv evening talk show.

An NBC chauffeur picked up Genie and her cofounder Claudia for a quick trip to Bloomingdale's to buy an outfit, (an electric green miniskirt).

Then there was the pre-interview, and the next night Genie was sitting next to Johnny while millions of Americans met the twenty-four-year-old Supergirl, from Mississippi.

Johnny seemed fascinated by Genie. He said she was "guileless." He held her and Claudia over for two segments while singers Pete Seeger and Peggy Cass paced in the Green Room.

The Girls were the hit of the advertising business. They staged exhibitions and dinners for agency clients. Supergirls peddled Eve cigarettes—the first ever female cigarette—on street corners. (Then, they considered it a breakthrough for women's rights.) They designed home meditation centers, refurbished private yachts, and uncovered a long-abandoned subway stop below Grand Central Station for a theater party.

Supergirls opened branches in Washington and Atlanta. The "Charlie's Angels" TV show was inspired by their chutzpa.

But in time, the business faded. Genie dreamed on. "I was a happy, sunny puppy dog," she remembered. She and Claudia wrote "Supergirls: the Autobiography of an Outrageous Business" for Harper and Row, and "The Woman's Guide to Starting a Business" for Holt that went into seven editions.

When I first met Genie, the Union Dime Bank had hired her to lecture on how women could get their lives in order and start a business—but her life was not in order. She was living out of a suitcase, house-sitting from apartment to apartment, between jobs.

Her best friend from childhood days in Kentucky had died in an attempt to fly the Atlantic Ocean in a balloon named *The Free Life*. Pamela Brown and her husband Rod had planned this flight after learning that it had never been done before. They dreamed of being the first. In the age of Vietnam, dropping out, and race riots, they drifted back to the nineteenth century with their balloon vision.

In America then, ballooning was not the sport it is today. Most had never seen such a sight outside of the Jules Verne film. Pam and Rod spent three years learning about ballooning, talking to balloonists, raising money, working with a lighter-than-air craft builder, and promoting the idea. They hired an experienced British balloonist to pilot and in 1970 they were ready to go.

Genie, along with hundreds of well-wishers, gathered in a field on the eastern tip of Long Island and waved goodbye as her friend ascended into the clear skies and headed off northward across Long Island Sound.

Thirty hours later, the balloon's pilot radioed the Coast Guard that they were caught in a freak storm off Newfoundland and descending fast. Then silence. Genie and a crew hired by Pamela's family searched the North Atlantic for two weeks after the Coast Guard had stopped. She later recounted going aboard every international fishing vessel harboured in St. Johns with photographs of the gondola and its passengers, but no one had seen anything. *The Free Life* left no trace.

She worked at the Museum of Modern Art as an events planner for their Picasso show; she was hired to write a book about bananas. People stopped her on the street and asked her for her autograph. But it was because she looked like Ellen Burstyn, who had just been nominated for an Academy Award. Sometimes she actually gave them an autograph. A cab driver, himself a would-be actor, was so certain she was Ellen Burstyn he locked the doors and said, "You're not getting out of this cab until you admit who you are." She confessed that he was right.

How could she tell him she was only the would-be author of a book about bananas? Banana history, banana recipes, banana growing, banana republics, banana jokes? *The Complete Book of Bananas.*

Genie came to New York with a dream. Now others dreamed her as somebody else.

I had come to New York as a failed novelist, and a fired Doubleday editor.

For both of us it was over.

My mother had willed me enough money for a small house, shelter I could no longer afford in New York. Far out on Long Island, I could bicycle to the post office, bicycle to the market, bicycle to the beach, bicycle to somewhere. We didn't call it marriage. We didn't call it anything.

In May 1981, we packed our few things into a small U-Haul truck and headed east down the Long Island Expressway.

Waiting for us was a dinky, dark summer cottage with bunk beds in two small bedrooms and a huge plywood bar that took up most of the kitchen.

The land around it was as spectacular as the house was depressing. The beach was a short walk down a dirt road, and on days with a northwest wind, the surf roared onto the sand and the bell buoy clanged. Through the budding trees we could see Long Island Sound, the same water that *The Free Life* had sailed over. We planned to become strong riding our bikes through these woods and swimming in the sound.

As we drove that last mile to the house, leaving New York forever, we passed under a bower of just-blooming dogwood blossoms.

The future was wide open, and soon to become rocky. And having a child was not even a notion.

Boys, sometimes you will arrive at a point where almost anything else can happen. Keep the faith and wait. A daughter may be on the way, twin boys—you don't know.

Not knowing is where we should be.

Not knowing is where we are, like it or not.

95% of the universe is unknown
and perhaps unknowable.
BH/Journal

I WISH, O SON OF THE LIVING GOD, O ANCIENT, ETERNAL KING, FOR A HIDDEN LITTLE HUT IN THE WILDERNESS THAT IT MAY BE MY DWELLING . . . FRAGRANT LEEK, HENS, SPECKLED SALMON, TROUT, BEES. RAIMENT AND FOOD ENOUGH FOR ME FROM THE KING OF FAIR FAME, AND I TO BE SITTING FOR A WHILE PRAYING GOD IN EVERY PLACE.

> 9th century Irish
> Hermit's Song

The Dalai Lama says he doesn't need any theology beyond kindness. "I'm just a simple monk. I'd like to make a small contribution."

Later on NBC in Barbara Walters' program on "Heaven," featuring priests, atheists, Islamic would-be suicide bombers, the Dalai Lama giggles (giggles!) "I'm only a teacher. I just want to be helpful." At program's end, Walters "with the permission of his holiness" kisses his cheek and he in turn enthusiastically rubs noses with her. "Eskimo kiss" he laughs. That's my kind of a god.

BH/Journal

Dear Boys,

Genie and I were almost certain we were too old to be parents. Genie had only the portion of an ovary as a result of a cyst operation years ago. But after much worry, marital uproar, and arguments, we gave it a try. Here is the moment that we learned the result of the pregnancy test and knew Lily lived. Someday I hope you guys have many such moments. Stay with the rough strife of your marriage. Keep the faith in each other. You too may have kids as lovely and loving as your mom.

*   *   *

For days the hospital said they had no word about Genie's pregnancy test. They were terribly busy, the assistant explained. In fact, at that moment Dr. Livoti, our doctor, was on an emergency caesarean.

For sure, they would telephone us tomorrow.

We sat near the phone the next day from eight to five.

At five, Genie called Livoti's office again. It was closing time, but a voice answered. When Genie complained, the voice said, "I'm only a temp."

"We've been waiting for two whole weeks! I have to know if I have a baby in me!" Genie cried.

"I think I saw a memo around here," the temp said. "We'll call tomorrow. I have to go home now."

"For the sake of all humanity," Genie pleaded, "if you have any sense of decency, look for that memo now!"

The temp said she'd try. She hung up.

"She won't ever call," Genie said. "It's nothing to them. Hundreds of tests a week. What can a temporary secretary care? Am I supposed to get down on my knees? Please let that phone ring."

Instantly it rang.

"The result is positive."

"Positive!" Genie shouted, and leaped up.

"Positive!" I cheered.

I kissed her cheek and held her and steadied her shaking hand. Together we hung up the phone.

It was July 19, 1983.

This might actually be happening, I thought.

Sophie, our Labrador, pranced into the room, begging a walk.

"We'll celebrate at Sophie's Beach!" Genie said.

Sophie's Beach was a long mud bank on a marshy inlet. Now and then local fishermen launched their boats there, and in the nights parked lovers used the dirt road leading up to it. But on this cool, gray evening with a drizzle falling, the three of us had it alone.

I brought along Sophie's supply of used tennis balls and a bottle of champagne. We set up a bar on the hood of the Chevy and toasted the universe, while Sophie jumped off the mud banks into the bay with gigantic splashes and paddled off to retrieve thrown balls. Sophie, our child.

The champagne was Genie's farewell to booze. She knocked it back, stripped down, and plunged into the inlet, naked.

"How do you feel?" I called through the drizzle.

"Incredibly high!"

Sophie splashed after more balls while Genie swam far out into the mist, her face up to the rain. I sat on the car hood and sipped.

Much later, soaking dog, towel-draped Genie, and I left Sophie's Beach in the twilight and headed toward her house.

Everything was about to change for us. Slowly I was beginning to hope that.

At this time Lily was a tiny speck, splashing in joy.

Dear Boys,

As often as I protest against needless and destructive technology, there are moments when new devices perform wonders.

After many months of pregnancy, Genie suddenly began to bleed profusely. We were sure it was a miscarriage and Lily was gone. Our doctor suggested that we try a new gadget called a Sonogram.

Driving us to New York, I wondered how Genie could hold back despair. I knew her womb was an empty space. There was nothing to see there with this new Sonogram invention.

We stopped. We started and stopped again. Just before noon we parked on East Sixty-Eighth Street outside of the laboratory that Dr. Livoti had directed us to.

A peppy nurse led us to the changing room.

I was told to be seated next to a stack of family magazines featuring happy moms and pops and kids. I wondered if I would throw up. This was just a wake, a technical wake, for your mom, who had vanished.

Now they were gazing at an empty place in Genie. Soon they would arrive and tell me the unfortunate news.

I was crippled with sorrow.

The nurse peeked around the corner of a partition. "Would you like to see your child?"

I had no idea what she was talking about. I stared at her.

"Would you like to see your child? Come with me." She motioned. I followed.

In a small room, Genie lay on a table with her belly exposed. Over her was a sort of grainy TV screen.

"Just watch the screen, said the doctor. She passed an instrument over Genie's middle and pointed out the features of her womb, a "over here, out of harm's way, here's your baby." She pointed at a tiny body with a head, two legs, and arms. Arms waving at us. Lily was waving! Hello, hello!

"Hello to you too," I gulped, and then I waved back at Lily.

My knees shuddered. I collapsed on a stool, wordless at the first sight of our resurrected child, your mom.

Later, Dr. Livoti mailed us the sonogram negatives: two sheets of eighteen black-and-white three-by-two-inch images. Lily lies in shadows on what seems like a moonlit beach, cushioned in sand dunes.

Dr. Livoti said the sonogram was a modern marvel. A few years before this, after so much bleeding, the child might have been scraped out at a local hospital in a routine D and C operation.

She called Lily "my sonogram baby."

Lord, make us instruments of your peace. Where there is hatred, let us sow love; where there is injury, pardon; where there is discord, union; where there is doubt, faith; where there is despair, hope; where there is darkness, light; where there is sadness, joy. Grant that we may not so much seek to be consoled as to console; to be understood as to understand; to be loved as to love. Amen.

Prayer of St. Francis

Dear Boys,

The birth of your mother changed our lives profoundly. From the very second Lily was lifted from Genie's womb by Caesarian operation, she was calm, and determined and at peace. Exactly as she is today.

You two guys are as lucky as any guys could ever be to have her as your mom.

It all began in Lenox Hill Hospital, New York City, 2:32 pm, March 14, 1984. Lily was serene.

Her dad, who had never held an infant, was terrified he would drop her.

I expected Lily would be wailing after the day's frenzy, but now she smiled slightly. Smiling about what? I asked myself in the recovery room.

Wondering at her face and eyes that now and then opened and drowsily shut again, I, like trillions of dads before me, simply worshiped my daughter. In her minuscule fingers, perfectly formed, I sensed divinity. How could such perfection be created from such a ridiculous pair of parents? Lily was palpable evidence of something greater than us.

In Lily's face I hunted for clues about her future. Did she resemble my mom? My shy pop? Genie's sad mother? Would she be like any of them? So far for you to go, Lily I thought, so far.

Finally, as the stapled-up Genie was wheeled in to caress her child, smiling through puffy lips, I worried: Will Lily like me?

I was astonished by the question. Like her dad?

I had become a boy again, desperate for the praise of women, once again huddled next to my dying mother's bed, waving my latest review in her eyes. As I cradled my daughter, I struggled to still the terrors in my mad, male heart.

Lily was calm about all that, as calm as my mother had been.

From the start, Lily took over our lives, and her own. I thought I would be busy nurturing her, an important fellow. But she fed at Genie's breast, slept most of the time in her profound calm, and grew strong. Aside from diaper duty now and then, I wasn't essential. If it weren't for Lily's welcoming smile, I might have felt useless.

Lily didn't just smile; she grinned in an open-mouthed *gaaaa* of hilarity. If she were sitting up, she'd often blast herself over backward with her *gaaaa* and lie in her bassinet flapping her arms like a tiny bird. She couldn't get enough of her visitors.

She looked hard at them, concentrating on their faces, studying them.

I wanted to talk with her, to know who she was, what she knew. I couldn't wait for her words.

When I had held the glass to my dying mother's lips, I felt so close, but so far away. What was it like to be dying? I had wanted to become my mother's mind.

Now, as I held a bottle to Lily's lips, I longed to know what it was like to be just born, to be so excited that almost any event set her to slapping both her knees in delight.

By the end of November, Lily was crawling about her playpen and standing by holding onto the bars. Genie and I noticed that when the radio was on Lily swayed to the music.

Lily was beginning to dance.

For months she stood in place, supported by her parents, bobbing and bouncing, clapping her hands, interpreting any rhythm available. When, with excited giggles, she walked alone for the first time, it was more an extension of her dancing than a new skill.

She seldom merely walked—she either ran or danced. She learned how to put a tape in the stereo and Genie and I would wake to her music from the living room downstairs, soon named "The Dance Room" by Lily. There she danced in front of a floor-to-ceiling mirror, perhaps imitating the bouncing ladies at Genie's exercise class.

Lily wasn't particular about her music—Beach Boys, Rolling Stones, or *Oklahoma!* were OK with her. But Gershwin's *Rhapsody in Blue* was her favorite. Usually naked, she interpreted Gershwin's nuances in precise coordination with arms, legs, head, her whole body, bounding and bowing with rolls and somersaults, slow, fast, graceful, manic, and always with an inspiration that knew no design or choreographer.

With dance she made peace. If Genie was moody or Daddy was fussy, Lily snagged us and pulled us into her 3 year old's dance room, where she insisted that we twirl and jump with her. She led, we followed. She was no easy instructor, and there was never any excuse for not dancing. Lily hounded her reluctant parents from room to room. "Dance! Dance, now!"—until we gave in and spun to her lead. I, who hadn't danced for years, now stooped to encircle her waist and learn all over again the lessons of rhythm.

Only once had I danced like Lily. Drunk, on a restaurant table, a college sophomore, I pranced and was glorious. I ate the flowered centerpiece. For Lily no booze was required, and it wasn't necessary to eat the flowers.

Summer evenings we took the radio to a bay beach and Lily danced with us or by herself in the sunset. When the moon rose she practiced the sound of her new word, *moooooooon*. She called out, reaching for it.

On winter evenings, Lily staged her own performances for us. Genie strung a sheet across the dance room and dimmed the lights. "Presenting Lily Henderson!" she called and we applauded as Lily entered, bottomless or in her pink tutu, from behind the sheet, bowing and waving into my flashlight beam. Lily liked the entrance almost as much as the dance and she'd return behind the sheet and reappear over and over until Genie coached, "It might be time for the show now, Lily." Then Lily was gone into *Rhapsody in Blue*, the entire two sides of the tape and asking to start over.

How did she know all of this? I am reminded of Wordsworth, ". . . trailing clouds of glory do we come/From God . . ." Genie remembered a friend who listened on the house extension as her four-year-old asked the infant in its crib upstairs, "Tell me about God. I'm beginning to forget."

Lily taught me again how to kiss. Her kiss asked for nothing, withheld no information, was given without reservation. It had no history, no future, wanted only the moment.

Because Lily's kisses carried no baggage, she soothed her Granny's last years. When she and Genie flew south, Lily ran helter-skelter to her Granny's wheelchair with greetings that knew nothing of her drinking or past agony.

When news came that Granny had died, Lily's kisses comforted Genie while my kisses could offer only reserved sympathies.

Lily was always mannerly. "Dank do," she'd say when given her bottle. "Bite?" "Sip?" she'd ask, wanting to share. "Hi you! Comere. Sit der," she'd greet a visitor to her play table.

"Hurt? Hurt?" she worried, touching the shin I'd just banged, or Genie's scalded finger, or the dog's stepped-on tail. In her question was the healing prayer.

Once when I lay on the sofa with fever, she constructed an elaborate ceremony for me on the rug with a jump rope, a chunk of chalk, her mittens, and a magic song. It worked. In the morning I was better.

When we passed a flattened rabbit on the road one Easter morning, I quipped, "Looks like the Easter bunny didn't make it this year."

She was on me immediately. "Not funny, Daddy."

"Sorry," I apologized to my indignant five-year-old. We rode in silence.

"I wonder how it happened?" Lily asked, noticing my sulking.

I shook my head.

"Not that you were there, Daddy," she added, freeing me from road-kill complicity. Later she admitted she never thought it was the *real* Easter bunny. In fact, she hadn't believed in that bunny, or in Santa Claus either. "You and Mom wanted me to believe, so I pretended to. I didn't want to hurt your feelings."

I worried about Lily's empathy for squashed bunnies, banged shins, scalded fingers, and stepped-on tails. I worried even more about the onslaught of erect boys that was only a few years away. She might be too tender for a world where kindness was a luxury.

Then I remembered the incident of the plastic scooter. Lily was about three. The scooter was bigger than she was and weighed more, too. She wanted to drag it into the house but she couldn't fit it through the sliding glass door. A wheel caught, or the handlebars. From the corner of the yard I watched her. Only a week before, she would have called for Daddy's help. But this matter was between herself, the scooter, and the door. She yanked, she twisted, she flipped that scooter, and she didn't complain. Some way the scooter was going in. Finally, she kicked it and it clattered into the house.

I saw that there was a core of Lily that was not to be messed with, by scooter or human.

One day that same year she learned the importance of her name.

"Hey, kid!" I called as she dashed across the yard.

She stopped, hands on hips. "Name's Lily," she yelled.

"OK, OK, Lily," I agreed, and never called her "kid" again lightly.

Soon the "Lily" was joined to a last name. "Name's Lily Hunnerson," she told guests as she considered them eye to eye.

And there was even more for her to be proud about two months later.

"Guess what, Daddy."

"I give up. What?"

"I'm a girl!" she shouted.

This was real news and she knew it immediately. Huge news.

Lily Hunnerson. A girl!

And tough enough to kick a scooter through a door without apologies.

Lily, like her mom, loved a joke. Any joke.

One afternoon, at our Maine summer house, she snuck up the steps to the loft where I was napping over a manuscript and pounced on me, sitting on my chest.

"Daddy, say after me."

"OK."

"Watta."

"Watta."

"Goose."

"Goose."

"Siam."

"Siam."

"What a goose I am, you said that." And she ran downstairs to tell Genie about her marvelous trick on Dad.

Her humor was far more scatological than I had been permitted as a boy. One morning we all lay in the summer predawn darkness and heard a bird begin to sing. The bird was creating an elaborate song, really working out, when he seemed to notice that he was all alone. The bird shut up and sang no more.

"Lily," I said, "that bird got up too early. He made a dope of himself. Now he's sitting out there in the dark all embarrassed and red-faced."

Lily hooted. And farted under the covers. Because of the fart, she hooted again. And farted again. She ran out of the room hooting and farting and hooting at the red-faced bird and her own embarrassment.

One morning Lily woke me quite early. "Daddy, come quick. It's 'mazing."

I didn't want to wake, but she whispered in my ear over and over, "It's 'mazing." She led her grumpy dad to her room.

A huge full moon was setting in the west and through another window the sun, even larger, was rising from the direction of the ocean at our backs.

I sat on her bed and shared her rapture.

Every year our little village put on a Halloween party for the children. When Lily was six, the minister's wife, dressed as a Gypsy fortuneteller, set up headquarters in a tent in the local hall. Lily dressed as a little witch with green hair and a hearth-side broom, entered the tent to have her palm read by the mysterious lady. The tent door flapped shut behind her, and the future was revealed to her.

Suddenly Lily plunged back out through the flap, losing her hat, shouting and running, her palms held out before her. "Mommy, Mommy, I'm so 'cited! The lady told me I'll have three babies when I grow up!"

She stared at the wonder in her hands and for a long time would not close them.

Lily sat on the toilet, thinking, while I shaved. "Sometimes I wonder what it's like to be another person."

"I wonder about that, too," I said. "I wonder what it's like to be you, Lily."

"What's it like to be you, Daddy?"

I put my razor down. Looking at her in the mirror, I attempted. "Well, most days I work at Pushcart Press in the garage. I make phone calls. Think up ideas for books. Write in my journal. Pack books in boxes."

"Oh," she said, reaching for the toilet paper.

"That's a very good question you asked, Lily."

Lily looked at me, flushed the toilet, and left without comment, perhaps already on to the next wonder, perhaps disappointed by my lame answer.

One August night on our Maine summer island, Genie, Lily and I drove to a hilltop cemetery to watch the annual Perseid shooting star showers. We lay on the blanket and stared upward together into the clear, cold sky.

It wasn't a great night for shooting stars, but the crickets were berserk with song.

"Sometimes I hear crickets sing and sing and then I sleep and they stop. I wake up because I can't hear them anymore. It's so quiet I wonder what happened to them," Lily commented.

We listened some more. "How do crickets sing, Dad?"

"Well, they rub their legs together . . ."

"But how does that make music?"

Long ago I had wondered about that too. But time had passed and I forgot to wonder, just as time rushed over the people buried in this cemetery and over the three of us sitting on this hillside watching for brief, sudden passages of light.

"I don't know," I said.

Simple wonders. The Blue Hill Fair. Home of Wilbur the pig and Charlotte and her web. A warm, windy Maine day. Lily and her friend Ellie sampling fried dough and cotton candy. Sheepdog trials and oxen pulls and bagpipers. And two lop-eared baby rabbits that Lily and Ellie adopted. And that twirling merry-go-round, Lily on a striped zebra, Ellie on a spotted giraffe. Protective parents standing next to them. Genie and her video camera outside the rail attempting to capture the moment. Lily and Ellie in timeless, whirling laughter as a giant pipe organ kept the beat.

"Dad, what will people say we did?" Lily asked me one afternoon as we were driving to the dentist for our checkups. Her class had just visited the town marine museum and its farming and fishing artifacts.

I had no answer. One hundred years from now what would we have left behind? "They'll say we drove cars, had children, lived in houses, got our teeth checked . . ."

"No. What will they say we *did*?"

"You know what it's called when you think about the past, Lily 'N-o-s-t-a-l-g-i-a'." I spelled it out for her. A new word, ducking the question. "Nostalgia is when you remember things. Like I remember you as a baby, still needing to get your diapers changed."

"Dad!" Lily scolded.

I shut up.

The dentist said our teeth were fine. But afterward, her question wouldn't leave me. Farm, fish? No, I decided: We bought stuff and sold stuff, that was the answer. All was for sale, all we cared about. Sex sold best. Would we leave behind plows and fishing gear? No. Only stuff—and lots of electronic gizmos.

People might note our busy lifestyle—a style that seemed to change from month to month, but a busyness that never changed as we rushed from place to place and fired off empty electronic messages.

Lily, I could have said, they might say we did nothing at all.

Lily resisted math, just as I had. Her teacher warned us that she was falling behind. Lily attended special classes after school to help her.

I told Lily that only her teachers needed help, not her. "Haven't I known you for seven years? How long have they known you? Two months?"

Lily complained and cried about math and, as my mother was for me, I was her tutor. We got through it and she made the honor roll.

"Just remember, Lily, I'm your best pal," I said.

"No, you're not. You are my Daddy."

Right again.

Adults made her sit through boring dinners and wouldn't let her eat Spaghettios. Genie insisted on combed hair and neat clothes. Daddy was a fanatic about brushing teeth. One night it all became too much and Lily kicked her foot against the wall, smashing clear through the wallboard. She hadn't known she was that strong and ran off to hide in a closet upstairs, terrified. "Gosh, you're strong," I said, comforting her and coaxing her out.

Another night she fled the adults into a rainy night, screaming, "I hate you, I hate you both and I always will . . . but I still love you."

Foot through the wall, screams in the rain. Even Lily at her worst was passionate.

Until Lily was born I didn't realize what true joy was—watching your child grow up, and learning from her again how to dance, and kiss, and make magic, and to feel sorrow about road-killed rabbits and laugh at silly jokes and fall into rapture about the setting moon and rising sun, and marvel at the mystery that might be hidden in your palm, and wonder about how crickets sing, and strut with pride at your gender and your very own name.

And above all to be constantly and forever amazed.

Boys, as a child, your mom knew about "love and wonder" long before I did. It might be tough to become "as a child," as Jesus said, especially as you are leaving your own childhood, but someday you will appreciate all that you have left and, I dare predict, you will value it all over again.

THE ENDLESS CYCLE OF IDEAS AND ACTION,
ENDLESS INVENTION, ENDLESS EXPERIMENT
BRINGS KNOWLEDGE OF MOTION BUT NOT
OF STILLNESS;
KNOWLEDGE OF SPEECH BUT NOT OF SILENCE;
KNOWLEDGE OF WORDS AND IGNORANCE OF
THE WORD.
ALL OUR KNOWLEDGE BRINGS US NEARER
TO OUR IGNORANCE—
WHERE IS THE LIFE WE HAVE LOST IN LIVING?
WHERE IS THE WISDOM WE HAVE LOST
IN KNOWLEDGE?
WHERE IS THE KNOWLEDGE WE HAVE LOST
IN INFORMATION?
THE CYCLES OF HEAVEN IN TWENTY CENTURIES
BRING US FARTHER FROM GOD
AND NEARER TO THE DUST.
T.S. Eliot

We worry about a paper cut on our little finger more than we are concerned about the millions of starving around the planet.

BH/Journal

Dear Boys,

Sometimes you will be at your lowest point. Then suddenly the blessings of The Great Mystery descend on you. Here is such a moment in my life.

In Maine, I built a house with my bare hands. No power tools at all, I liked to brag. Just a hammer, handsaw, and a T-square. Lily called the old well on the property a "whale," so we named it the Lily Whale House. I was too impatient in 1991 to install Sheetrock interior walls at the Whale House. I resisted the idea of taping and sanding Sheetrock to a fussy finish, so I nailed up real pine paneling. Manly country stuff.

It was on this paneling that Lily banged her head with an awful wallop while bouncing on her bed. Days later she complained suddenly of an excruciating headache and we rushed her to the Island Medical Clinic where the doctor tested her reflexes, flashed lights in her eyes, and advised us to get an immediate CAT scan at the Ellsworth Hospital.

Genie and I placed her on the back seat. I was certain that at any moment Lily would die from a blood clot as we sped north over narrow, blind-crested country roads to the hospital an hour north.

I swore to myself if Lily died I would kill myself. There was no other reason to live. I'd take my chances on finding her again in the afterlife. By night, I too would be dead.

Later, Genie told me she had planned the same for herself. Then Grace descended.

Grace.

From nowhere, unsought, and inappropriately. Lily was dying. I was doing eighty miles an hour. And this thing happened.

I suddenly felt an enveloping love for the entire universe. Not just for my suffering child. For Genie. For all of it. For all our living and dying.

And I knew I was loved in return. From the very depth of the stars, I was loved.

There would be no suicide.

After the CAT scan, the doctor said Lily was OK, and Genie and I collapsed in relief.

And Love became palpable.

Grace had transcended Lily and Genie and me and infused every pebble on the road as we tore desperately toward Ellsworth.

Dear Boys,

Sometimes your life will change in an instant. And often after a tragedy a way will open over time to joy. The Great Spirit, God, or The Great Coincidence will take control. Try to keep that hope.

E.B. White once said "A really companionable and indispensable dog is an accident of nature. You can't get it by breeding and you can't buy it with money. It just happens along."

Over my eighty years I have been the companion for many such dogs. In my older age, Lulu was my indispensable pal. For ten years we were never apart.

After the death of Lily's beloved beagle Opie under a truck's wheels, I met Lulu at the local Animal Rescue Fund shelter, where she resided under the name of Chewy.

Chewy had been at the shelter for more than a year, unclaimed, unloved—a single mom, spayed now. Had her profligate motherhood driven her from her previous home? About two years old? Nobody knew for sure.

She was about eighty-five pounds of shagginess. Perhaps a committee had pieced her together—a German shepherd face, floppy dreadlocked Afghan ears, a golden retriever body. Her face and muzzle said ferocious, her eyes indicated kind, her tail wagged like a puppy's for friend and stranger alike.

I have known few animals—and fewer humans—with such a natural, unselfconscious dignity. She accepted me and I her with no question. We walked and thought in tandem. At the ARF office, I asked for permission to take Chewy home for an overnight, so Lily and Genie could approve of her. I filled out some papers, made a small donation. She walked alongside me to the car, and I opened the door. She looked back at me. "You want me to get in?" she asked with her eyes. "Go ahead, Chewy. Let's meet some people," I replied.

At home, Lily and Genie were weeding in the garden, getting all in order for the summer renters. When I walked through the gate with Chewy, Genie's immediate response was, "Oh no, you don't!" She wanted to properly mourn Opie and at least wait through the summer before getting another dog.

"Just for one night?" I asked. "I'll take her back tomorrow." I let her off the leash, and she circled the yard, tail down, head down, nervous. She'd been penned up for a long time. I worried she'd run away or turn nasty. We all sat and watched. Eventually, she completed her rounds and returned to me. She took the leash in her mouth, wagged her tail, and said with her eyes, "I am your friend. I am the one you've been looking for." Then she laid her head on my shoulder. Genie gasped. "What have they been training those dogs to do over at ARF?" she said, but she was laughing.

That evening, Chewy went with us to two lawn parties. At one she fetched the host's newspaper for him. At another she bounded around the lawn with such glee that the hostess was alarmed for her wine glasses and trays of crudités. "That dog is not trained!" she screeched.

I took Chewy home, glad to be free of the East Hampton summer inanities and soon off to Maine. Could she stay?

First we had a family discussion. At breakfast Chewy was the quintessential diplomat, making the rounds of the table, her head on our knees, looking at each of us with her deep, kind eyes. Never begging for food. Chewy never begged for anything.

Yes, we voted. She could stay. But that name. Did she chew up stuff as a puppy? Was that still her hidden fault? In any case, "Chewy" didn't fit.

"How about Louie?" I suggested. Louie sounded like Chewy, and she might be more comfortable with it.

"She's a girl, Dad," Lily, reminded me.

"A single mom," Genie added.

"How about Floozy?" I tried.

"Not funny, Dad."

"I know," said Genie. "My favorite comic book character. Lulu. Little Lulu."

So it was—Chewy to Louie to Lulu, which didn't fit her either, but it avoided a radical change in her name.

Within days, Lulu and I were off to Maine to open up the tower and the cabin for the summer.

Farley Mowat, in his dog memoir, *The Dog Who Wouldn't Be,* about his mutt called "Mutt," states of the great plains of western Canada, "The prairies could be only half real to a boy without a dog." That's how it was for me with Lulu in our Maine wilderness.

Bear country was everywhere around us—miles and miles of it. Big, old black bears rolled in the summertime blueberry fields out back scooping up paws of berries; they fled in terror when Lulu trotted down the road (hunters used dogs to chase bears—why hunt bears? To kill a big thing, that's why, stupid). Lulu would have preferred to play with the bears, but they weren't that silly.

Still, they didn't like to be surprised. Moms with cubs could be very nasty. So on our daily four-mile hike down to the post office and back, I would have loud conversations with Lulu, or I would sometimes sing to warn the bears that we were about. Lulu and I would return with our mail, rest halfway on a blueberry knoll and check out the clouds, the sun, or the fog, swatting some flies, and head on back up the hill, talking and singing. Once a bear crossed the road, apparently not hearing our approach. He regarded us and silently hurried off. Lulu wished he had stayed.

One day at the top of the hill while waiting for Lulu to pee, I looked into a deep ditch and saw a huge bear seemingly asleep, his back up against a tree, head lolling as if drunk or hung over. We left. The next day he was still there, dead for sure. Hit by a car, said the game warden later, but I suspected he'd been shot for kicks.

The Frost Pond was our secret adventure many summer afternoons. (In Maine lakes are called ponds, with typical Down East understatement.) Even some locals knew nothing of this pure lake hidden away down a rough dirt road, lost in woods and blueberry fields. On our hikes there, Lulu and I met only eagles and turkeys and deer and now and then a coyote or a porcupine, which Lulu was wise enough to avoid. The pond was her huge pleasure. She'd dive off the bank into the clear water and watch me with delighted eyes, paddling herself cool.

When she was still young enough, we'd head off deeper into the woods, marking our return trail with bits of paper, having no compass or other sensible gear that any Boy Scout would pack. The woods were laced with old logging trails. We followed them here and there singing out for the bears (and more dangerous, a mad moose). My favorite tune, for some reason, was from Disney's *Snow White,* the dwarfs' "Whistle While You Work." Whistling and singing, we covered many miles. It seemed to me that nothing could ever ruin our land; there was simply too much of it. New houses sprouted up here and there, but many old houses were likely to go unclaimed and collapse into their cellar holes, where nature embraced them again.

Our insane national infatuation with growth at all costs didn't apply. The GDP was at slack tide here.

The blueberry fields that surrounded the cabin had been nurtured and raked for hundreds of years. The streams ran pure; the rough gravel and stone beaches were unspoiled by the tourists; and the village looked the same as it had for centuries.

Lulu and I imagined that this was truly home.

In the evenings, before she became too old, Lulu chased tennis balls up and down the dirt road in front of the tower. Then I sipped some wine, and we sat next to each other in the tall grass and felt twilight descend around us.

We talked in silence. If I was depressed for some reason, she sat beside me and licked my hand. "Thanks, Lulu," I'd say and know it was all better for now.

Summer to summer, with Lily often at camp or at school, Lulu and I were kids together. And summer to summer, without really noticing it, we grew old together.

The heat began to get to aging Lulu, and she hid under the cottage many July days. Our trips to the post office and to the Pushcart bookstore were more often by Oldsmobile than foot. We also drove halfway to the Frost Pond and sometimes merely climbed a nearby hill there to worship Acadia Park's mountains and the sea together. Hands out and palms open, I blessed those mountains and gently stirring ocean, and Lulu and I were blessed in return.

To the very end—winter or summer—Lulu loved the water. Her great joy was a robust splash, even into icy slush, as she retrieved a stick or a ball. Time and time again she'd ask for another toss, and I'd have to stop before she exhausted herself. On hot summer days, if I walked down the hill to the Pushcart bookstore or post office, I'd often try to sneak through the woods and leave her behind, fearful of the heat. But she'd always hear a leaf rustle or a twig snap, and she'd bound from under the house, ready to roll.

Lulu was somewhere near eleven or twelve, and I was well into my sixth decade. Our whiskers were turning gray and then white, our bellies filling out.

When Lulu was diagnosed with breast cancer—about the same time I was—some friends, including my oncologist, found my depression over her dying hard to understand. My cancer I could deal with, not Lulu's. It's just a dog, I heard in their muted sympathy.

My friend Rob McCall, the Congregational minister, understood about Lulu and me, about our perfect wordless conversations.

"Lulu and I talk about important stuff: about running on blueberry fields, the weather, chasing sticks and balls and food. Lulu loves to eat. She eats just about anything, unfortunately."

"I'm sure you don't talk about theology, then." Rob laughed.

"Nope, just the important stuff."

Rob knew there was no need for theology with Lulu. She was unconditional love, dog as god spelled backward. A cliché, I know, but the sentiment survives because it has always been true.

Our last hike in Maine was into a gold October valley, over maroon blueberry fields to the Frost Pond. Lulu swam, and I just lay on the field and watched the clear sun-washed sky and wondered if anything would ever be this perfect again.

That winter Lulu wanted to die alone and hidden. Twice she ran off into the night after I had let her out to pee.

The first time, when she didn't respond to my constant call, I worried that she had found a hole or shed to do her dying in, but at 2:00 a.m., suddenly she was standing outside the door, too weak to bark or scratch. I let her in with cries of welcome for a friend resurrected.

For a few days she showed signs of recovery, scrambling into the car for rides to the beach, eating with customary vacuum-cleaner lust. But on the night of a March snowstorm, three days before she died, she again ran off into the woods and ignored my calls. After midnight, Genie was shutting off the lights when she spotted Lulu standing in the snow motionless, coated with ice, a white ghost. Again we welcomed her back as if resurrected. But in the nights ahead she could not sleep, panting constantly and moving from spot to spot every few minutes because of her pain.

On March 10, the date my father died, I took Lulu for her last trip to the vet, still uncertain about what to do. The vet said it was time. Lulu didn't notice the injection into her rump. She quietly lay down on a quilt while the doctor, nurse, and I patted her and told her how very loved she was.

Her death hit me like a horrible physical pain. I barely made it out of the vet's office, and on the way home I became a sobbing road menace.

In the spring I scattered her ashes on the Frost Pond shore, the site of our last perfect day.

YOU THINK DOGS WILL NOT BE IN HEAVEN?
I TELL YOU THEY WILL BE THERE LONG
BEFORE ANY OF US.
Robert Louis Stevenson

. . . I am most immoderately married. The Lord God has taken my heaviness away. I have merged, like the bird, with the bright air, and my thought flies to the place by the bo-tree. being, not doing, is my first job.

Theodore Roethke

When we carry our small suffering in solidarity with the one universal longing of all humanity, it helps keep us from self-pity or self-preoccupation. We know that we are all in this together, and it is just as hard for everybody else. *Almost all people are carrying a great and secret hurt, even when they don't know it.* When we can make the shift to realize this, it softens the space around our overly defended hearts. It makes it hard to be cruel to anyone. Shared struggle somehow makes us one—in a way that easy comfort and entertainment never can.

Fr. Richard Rohr

Dear Boys,

I have often thought of publishing a book called "silence." Inside the book would be only empty pages.

Listening was easy on our Maine hill. When the wind was still and the birds and crickets and humans and coyotes were sleeping you could hear your ears humming. It was that silent. Visitors from the cities or suburbs found the quiet scary at first. The Holy Spirit moved about the forests and fields and over the stirring Atlantic and in the distance the eternal mountains sloping to the sea.

One August night in 2002, I sat on my cabin's porch swing with Lulu and watched the full sturgeon moon rise from behind Acadia National Park's mountains, and right beside it was Mars, now a mere 34 million miles from earth, as close as it had been in 60,000 years. The moon broadcast a shimmering path between the sea islands and out to the horizon. Mars was a hot red, and strangely comforting. The solar system had come so close, embracing almost. I looked for the craters of Mars, I waved at Mars, Ridiculously I called "howdy" in the quiet.

And together Mars and the moon continued to quietly rise together, a dance of grace and precision.

Not since 60,000 years—why was I blessed to witness this silent dance? I wondered.

I suggest that silence be a part of your daily routine.

THE MIND THAT IS NOT BAFFLED IS NOT EMPLOYED.
Wendell Berry

You must know that joy is more rare, more difficult and more beautiful than sadness. Once you make this all important discovery, you must embrace joy as a moral obligation.

André Gide

LILY'S BEATITUDES (age 3)
Blessed are they who are constantly amazed
As the moon rises.
Blessed are they who dance
Before they can walk.
Blessed are they who kiss
Without asking for a kiss.
Blessed are they who feel the hamster's pain
Before their own.
Blessed are they who are proud
To be a girl.
Blessed are they who laugh
Because farts are hilarious.
Blessed are they who remember Wordsworth's
"Trailing clouds of glory
do we come from God."
Blessed are they for whom love is
As real as a rock.

Dear Boys,

When I was a younger man, a middle age semi-geezer, I had the notion that I must build a tower in Maine. Here's how the tower came about, in case you guys ever want to erect a tall structure on your own. Never surrender your instinct to dream nice dreams.

After years of being written, more of being rewritten (every comma had to be correct, every memory exact), and many rejections, my latest memoir had finally been accepted by a publisher in Boston. I drove there, delivered the manuscript to Faber and Faber, and headed north to Maine, the balance of Faber's modest advance check in my pocket. I needed to see Maine again. I was emptied out. Lily was no longer a child; our baby didn't need her dad as much anymore. Memoir finished, baby gone, I felt hollow inside. Restless. Perhaps more depressed than I realized.

The real estate agent gave me general directions to Christy Hill. I asked for help at the Sedgwick general store and was told to circle the Baptist church and head straight up. Since the hill is almost 400 feet high, I expected a dramatic rise from sea level, but my ascent was a gradual one of soft inclines and plateaus through a mixed forest of spruce and maple, beech and birch.

Up I drove for another mile until the road peaked in an expanse of blueberry fields. Hearing my rackety car, three deer bounded across the white fields. The sun's glare off the snow made it hard to see, but finally I spotted the broker's sign that marked the lot, swinging on its hinges in the wilderness.

I stopped the car, and Opie our dog at the time, and I got out to look around. In the clear cold air to the northeast was the crown of Blue Hill, lofting over Blue Hill village at its base, scene of the annual Blue Hill Fair. Twenty miles to the east across Blue Hill Bay were the mountains of Acadia National Park, and below me were Swans Island and dozens of lesser islands and ledges, fringed with ice. Beyond them the open ocean stirred quietly.

I walked through the woods 160 feet to the stone wall at the rear of the lot, where I discovered more acres of blueberry fields and, miles away, light fog rising off the Penobscot River and, still farther in the distance, the mountains of the northwest.

I sat on that old stone wall for a long time, stunned by this sacred place.

There was no way I could afford it, I thought. My advance would cover only a portion of the asking price. Besides, what was this really but a 1.78-acre subdivision in the middle of nowhere?

More importantly, how could I explain this infatuation to Genie. She might point out that we already had the summer cottage on Deer Isle that I had spent years building obsessively. No way did we need another lot in Maine, she'd say, perhaps rising to operatic hyperbole about my edifice complex. She might remind me that we often couldn't pay our bills, particularly that fuel bill last winter. She would bring to my attention my dying Oldsmobile station wagon with more than 160,000 miles on the odometer, held together with duct tape. And I'd have to admit that while Pushcart Press had become an institution—with dozens of titles on its list and the Pushcart Prize being proclaimed by *The New York Times Book Review* as "a distinguished annual literary event"—the press had been hanging on by its financial fingernails for twenty-three years. Frequently I had relied on a cash miracle or the kindness of friends to bail it out.

"What would I do with this lot?" I asked myself on that wall.

"I called Doris Grumbach, at her bookstore nearby. She and her partner, Sybil, had lived here more than a decade. I invited Doris to church, and after church I drove her to the top of Christy Hill and pointed out the distant views across the fields.

"What are you going to do here?" Doris asked.

"I don't know. Probably leave it as it is. It's perfect. No houses, no people, wild."

Doris, who was always careful with her words, said nothing.

In my mind suddenly was a vision of a tower on a moonlit cliff—right out of some forgotten nineteenth-century romantic English novel that my parents or grandparents might have read. I didn't tell Doris about my vision. She might have questioned my taste, if not my sanity. A nineteenth-century tower? What could that possibly mean?

"Maybe I'll build a tower here." I laughed and started the car.

* * *

In the months before I discovered my tower lot on Christy Hill, a plague of cancers had suddenly descended on several of my friends, all of them young women. Their suffering devastated their families and all of us. Who could have faith in a universe that allowed this? Their agony was one of the reasons I had to lose myself in raising the tower. It became a tower of oblivion. Building, I didn't have to think constantly of horror, outrage, and terror.

My friend Kim was thirty-eight, kind, dark-haired, lovely, and the mother of three children—two girls, aged three and five, and a boy, eight. She had met her husband, Ken, when she was a student at Barnard and he at Columbia. After graduating, they married and moved to Southampton. He started a construction company and Kim worked as a personal care nurse.

Ken had almost finished building a house for his family when Kim's headaches started. An operation revealed an aggressive type of brain cancer. Doctors gave her a year at the most.

Kim knew the odds. She had witnessed her own patients die from this cancer. But for her kids and her husband, she never thought of quitting. The pain was constant, the five additional operations excruciating. She allowed herself to be used as a guinea pig for massive chemotherapy doses, without effect. A few months before she died, defying her cancer one last time, she ran, biked, and swam in a triathlon along the local roads and in the bay. At her death, she lay blind and unable to move, surrounded by her family, in the bedroom of the new house that Ken had just completed for her.

Kim had directed that no mention of God or religion be permitted at her funeral. Instead, in a hall packed with mourners, her friends recited her favorite words by Laurie Colwin, Anne Raver, E. B. White, and Kathleen Norris, and sang her favorite songs. As we filed out we all received Kim's final gift to us, a bar of the See's chocolate that she loved.

When I first heard of Kim's cancer, I hit the floor, pleading with the old God of my father's church. "This kind of thing just can't happen to anybody so young, so good. Her kids need her, her husband is wrecked," I explained to this God. I hadn't prayed since I was an adolescent.

On my knees I tried to think of a deal for this old God, the one who parted the Red Sea, whose Son healed the leper and raised Lazarus. The pal of Oral Roberts, Pop's radio healer. I pleaded: "If you heal Kim, I will become a born-again Christian and dedicate my life to your church. No questions asked."

There. My cards were on the table. It was the only thing I could think of. I waited for an answer of some sort. Silence.

When I stood up I felt dirty. I had just treated that God as though he were a car salesman hankering for a deal. I was suddenly appalled by my prayer, and then terrified by what may have been a degrading blasphemy of the very God I was beseeching. I

resolved to pray no more. After four decades without much praying, I had forgotten how to pray in any
case. What would come of my attempt to reach
God? I endured a low-grade fever of dread.

A few months later, an answer of sorts: My
brother Bob called me from Philadelphia. He said
his wife, Debbie, forty-four, an artist, teacher, and
community leader, mother of their two children, a
boy fourteen and a daughter eighteen, had also just
been diagnosed with brain cancer. It wasn't the
aggressive strain that was quickly killing Kim, but,
as Debbie's doctor said, "It kills you in the end."

Debbie was operated on at the University of Pennsylvania Hospital. She was left partially paralyzed
on her left side, unable to walk without assistance,
and doomed to spend her days on the living room
couch in front of the TV, swallowing dozens of pills
daily, doped and bloated. Bob slept on a rug on the
floor by her side, in constant attendance.

"Don't let them do this to you, Bill," she told
me after her operation. She also joked that she
would outlive her surgeon, who drove a new orange
Porsche, purchased, she assumed, with fees from that
operation.

Was this God's answer to my botched prayer?

When I told Genie about the deal I had offered God and the result, she observed dryly: "That makes you pretty important, doesn't it?"

Genie was mystified by me and losing patience with our constant poverty. We had been through many bad patches before, but this was starting to look like the end. I slept on the couch every night, alone and miserable.

Genie was right of course. How ridiculous to think my feeble prayer and Debbie's cancer were related, and how egomaniacal.

Kim, who became a hero to me, consoled Debbie by phone. Listless from chemotherapy and radiation treatments, Debbie had tired of talking to her desperate, helpless brother-in-law and friends, but for hours she discussed new chemicals and drugs, doctors, and all the exotica of brain cancer, with Kim.

When I offered what little solace I knew of to Kim, it was Kim who tried to cheer me up. Wearing a scarf to cover her bald head but looking just as young and alert as before her first operation, she held my hand: "Bill, we are all dying. I'm just getting there a little faster than the rest of us."

Every day became incredibly precious to Kim and Debbie. Dying, they loved living with an intensity that we healthy sorts lacked, and I lacked even more as ghastly news arrived of more friends' cancers: the young mother of one of Lily's best friends had colon cancer; another family friend had breast cancer. By the end of the year, three more women friends, all of them vital, good people, were diagnosed with various cancers.

What was the meaning of this grotesque chronology of misery? My huckster's prayer had nothing to do with it, of course, of course. But I didn't dare whisper a plea to heaven, even a plea for forgiveness for my original prayer.

As Simone Weil said in her own dark night, God was "more absent than a dead man, more absent than light in the utter darkness of a cell."

Sudden episodes of pure horror swept over me. Perhaps Yeats's rough beast, its "gaze blank and pitiless as the sun," was no longer slouching toward Bethlehem to be born. The beast had already arrived, indeed had always been in Bethlehem.

Lily's love might not be at the heart of the universe. Something terrible might be, and I was just beginning to see its malevolent face.

I was losing my balance in a new, more virulent form of vertigo. I had to do something just to remain standing on the ground. The "tower for no reason" became that something.

For three summers I labored on my tower structure, without power tools or help, just me, my dog, and the howling blueberry wilderness.

At the end of the third summer I stood 18 feet off the rocks and 400 feet above sea level on that hill. I peered into the twilight through my huge yard sale windows to both sea and mountains, hoping to spot a final shooting star. But the Perseid showers were done for the summer.

Straight up, a bald eagle nonchalantly suffered the attacks of two indistinct lesser birds that it had somehow offended. Tiring of them, the eagle dove in a sort of roll toward me, its immense wings churning down a wall of rushing air.

A mass of weighty clouds poured over the western mountains, for a time promising rain, but delivering only a spectacular sundown of pale Maine yellow and thunderous black. Below the sunset the stacked blue buckets waited in the string-lined fields.

Hints of grace were here, tumults of gratitude that knocked me suddenly to my knees in thanksgiving to a nameless, unnameable something. For what? For this, for all of it. To witness those clouds and mountains, that sun, the eagle, to have been granted more than fifty years to do just this. I was no longer a writer or publisher or any other definable entity. I was free from words, and bowed down by simple thanks.

Dostoevsky in "The Grand Inquisitor," from *The Brothers Karamazov*: Jesus has returned to earth and has been captured by the established Church. The Grand Inquisitor tells Jesus He did His work a long time ago, but now He'd better not contradict modern Church doctrine, or He'll get another taste of the cross. Did Jesus have anything to say for Himself?

"The Inquisitor falls silent, he waits for a certain amount of time to hear what his Captive will say in response. He finds His silence difficult to bear. He has seen that the Prisoner has listened to him all this time with quiet emotion, gazing straight into his eyes, and evidently not wishing to raise any objection. The old man would like the Other to say something to him, even if it is bitter, terrible. But He suddenly draws near to the old man without saying anything and quietly kisses him on his bloodless, ninety-year-old lips. That is His only response."

BH/Journal

Our choice is love or despair. The argument for love? There is no argument for love. Love is nonrational, defiant faith. Love is constant caring, reverence, and wonder at each tremendous second.

Despair's argument? It's rational and submissive. We are born of a chance encounter of sperm and egg. We struggle to grow and reproduce and then we die. Our star will one day incinerate our earth and all evidence of us. Despair is boredom, carelessness, depression, madness.

There is only one sin and that is the failure to love.

Since we all constantly fail to love, we forgive ourselves and others always.

Love is God. The kingdom of that God is within you and all persons, always.

BH/Journal

"The fundamentalist devotees of any religion will insist that their scriptures and traditions are the only true ones and that all others are false. They will insist that they have the whole answer, and unless you believe as they do, you are doomed. But around here, it's nearly impossible to make that case, as much as some still try.

"To see the limits of the orthodox view, just walk outside. See the round wreathes of balsam fir carefully constructed in the fertile female shape of the circle, as they have been for thousands of years. See the fir trees set up in so many homes, the ageless emblem of male power. These are symbols of the Old Faith, far older than any organized religion. See the tracks of the smaller creatures in the snow writing their truth in a strange, runic scripture that can be read, yes, but only by the fearless. Feel the cold wind from the frozen North, or the drear, wet wind from the East off the Great Water. Hear the last geese high above honking and beating their way South. See the lights in the windows of the white houses and the white churches with their long spires reaching heavenward topped by weathervanes pointing to the four directions. See the sun start its sojourn back up toward the peak of the heavens and feel the gut-deep joy at the returning of the light. Hold a new baby in its little snowsuit, hat and mittens, and know something no theology can teach. Know that here no one religion can ever contain or explain the truth of this overwhelming Creation: present, past, nor future. Know that the true believer and the fundamentalist hide out in fear of the real, wild world, dripping, dying, breathing, bleeding, melting, freezing, birthing, and healing; wholly created, wholly free, wholly original, wholly authentic . . . Wholly Holy."

Blue Hill Maine
First Congregational Church

ALL CHILDREN SMILE IN THE SAME LANGUAGE.
Dorothy Galloway

Dear Boys,

After I built the Tower, your mom helped me on another dreamer's project—a sacred space. Here's how.

For several years I was married to Nancy, the ex-nun who had fled the convent, left Princeton Graduate School, and eventually ditched me. But in 1971 we spent months living in poverty in the basement of a Normandy farm house and writing books.

When we were down to our last savings, we decided to spend it all on bus trips to the cathedrals of Beauvais, Amiens, Eure, Toulouse and finally Chartres.

Nancy, now an angry atheist, was unimpressed by most of the cathedrals. She and her former faith were not on speaking terms. But even she wasn't prepared for that first vision of Chartres.

We had been gazing out the bus window at the flat cornfields of Beauce with little interest when suddenly in the distance we saw something that just shouldn't have been there—an immense edifice, the whole works lifting into the sky like an improbable and sudden shout.

Years later that shout became an inspiration for building, with Lily's help, my own cathedral in the woods of Maine near the cabin and the tower.

Finishing that monument became my salvation while I recovered from cancer, 2005 to 2007.

Knowing far less than the master builders of Chartres, I planned my own leap into the sky, with my own honorary Christians in glass and stone. My family, my friends, my neighbors—these would be my honored saints.

I would build my cathedral on this hill over a long time. I imagined there was no rush. Indeed the idea of rush was anathema to me. Rush was what I had come to Maine to escape.

My cathedral would not imitate Chartres. It would be my own. My *"cathedra"* or bishop's seat would be there—as it is in all cathedrals big or small. It is where the bishop sits his butt. My butt.

I would build it as high as I could, using stone found in the woods and blueberry fields, with my own two hands. How high? I had no idea. In fact I'd never laid so much as a brick before, knew nothing about mortar or fitting one rock to another so that the entire pile didn't descend on the faithful below, but something was going to rise on this 3½ acre lot I owned, and it would be my idea of holy.

One day Lily and I had come upon a small rock outcropping. "It just felt right" Lily said later. She began to peel back the rock's moss cover. I joined in and we soon realized that this was no piddling stone but a substantial boulder.

We set to work with a pick ax, shovel, hammer and saw and soon uncovered a relatively flat oval ledge, cracked in the middle like a broken heart. The break between the two halves of the heart formed a natural pew on one side and an altar on the other.

This spot, alone in the woods, seemed miraculous to Lily and me—the perfect cathedral foundation. Until now this ledge had never seen the light, perhaps for thousands of years.

Words cannot touch what that foundation meant to us. Something holy had been buried and resurrected.

But what shape the cathedral? A modified cross like Chartres? No. Round. It had to be round. All the churches of my youth had been rectangles—the simple summer chapel in Ocean City, New Jersey; the pretentious boxed Bryn Mawr Presbyterian church in suburban Philadelphia where, of a Sunday, Rolls Royces and their chauffeurs waited for their worshipping bosses.

In such chapels and churches I had learned a boxed doctrine. Heaven is for the saved (us)—everybody else burns forever. A tidy package as long as you didn't try to exit the box.

A round structure implied an eternal circle of questions. There would be no neat corners for cute theology in a round cathedral. Besides, the box is unnatural. In nature there were few boxes—the moon, the sun, the earth, tree trunks, all round. A box was an anathema in all I saw around me.

But round was for sure. Round was revealed, slowly, under the hardscrabble that Lily and I had hacked away—the round, broken heart. I am still amazed by what Lily and I found on those late summer days when sea winds swept the mosquitoes from the woods and let us tear at the earth in peace.

Lily approved of my round concept. Hers was a round theology. At college in Northampton, Massachusetts she attended both a Quaker meeting and a Unitarian Church. "That makes me a Quackertarian," she smiled.

No boxes there.

* * *

I imagine our broken-hearted cathedral and our ring of rocks enduring the frigid brutality as they had for thousands of years, and would continue to do so for centuries more. After the cathedral toppled into ruins, a hunter or hiker might come upon the pile and realize somebody had built something here—a round something, certainly the circle indicated an impractical something. Perhaps an academic—if such still existed—would write a paper on it, a treatise on 21st century sun worship, a Druid revival, a burial pit. The academic wouldn't realize some of the rocks had names: "Lily" "Genie" and more local saints, with their stones.

For now, it endures. Inside, only a small wooden cross, the remains of a lobster trap donated to our effort by Doris Grumbach. *The New York Times* devoted a full-page feature with photos. Neighbors pass by and wonder about this odd guy from away.

Hope and despair alternated through those cancer years, while we built the cathedral.

When Simon & Schuster's Free Press sent me galley proofs of my hymn book memoir, now titled *Simple Gifts,* I scoffed at my sermonizing there. Hymns were no help now. I considered myself a religious bullshitter and a mere Preacher Boy. For over sixty years I'd had it easy. "You haven't even begun to suffer," I noted in the journal. And I was right. I'd been a privileged word slinger.

I diligently corrected the proofs but my inspiration for the book had vanished.

All churchy chatter and ceremony seemed ridiculous. God talk was just a Scrabble game for career Christians trying to beat the board with fancy words.

Only the Catholic crucifix of the suffering Jesus drew me in. The empty Protestant cross seemed empty indeed. That Catholic guy hanging there knew what it was like.

During those cancer years I sought a recovery of simple faith. There was no way else to go but back to what mattered.

What mattered now was a steel band street dance in the nearby town of Stonington. A Jamaica-inspired assembly of local amateur musicians let loose. Flatlanders and locals cut a rug, as did Lily and I, flailing like flappers in hilarious Sufi joy.

What mattered too was a canoe adventure on the Frost Pond just over the hill from our cathedral site. A bright, windy day on clear, robin's egg blue water—Lily and I paddled into the wind one way and snapped open a red, yellow and orange umbrella for a free ride returning, the wind at our back, laughing. And always there was the cathedral to build.

I told Doris Grumbach what the name Jesus meant to me during chemo and how the phrase "It's not about you," freed me.

"It's like you realized possibility again," she says.

Indeed I was free from my own tired proclamations, my own husk.

Last two weeks of Cancer radiation. Left chest a burned steak. Hair returning slowly—a crew cut. Went to Church, first time in six months. Old Tom Collins, not seeing me in pew, asks for an "update on Bill Henderson."

"Tom, I'm here! My hair's back!" I call from across the sanctuary.

Old militant patriot Tom. WWII vet. American flag flapping from his SUV antenna. A man whose politics I could dislike. And it's he who cared about me, and waves welcome.

Afterwards I tell the pastor what I had left deep into chemo was the name of Jesus and the words, "It's not about you."

Pastor Joe says, "That about sums it up for me too."

BH/Journal

Cancer Notes, 3rd Surgery

The idea of death became very real, but so did the love that friends, doctors, and nurses brought to me. As Emily Dickinson wrote: "That love is all there is/Is all I know of love."

Ego was obliterated. "Self" seemed silly, a pasted-together mirage. The real was exactly what St. Francis said it is: "In the giving of ourselves we receive, and in dying we're born to eternal life."

Faith I didn't know I had, from my childhood, bred in the bone, carried me through those long, often confusing and depressing months of consultations and treatment that followed.

Since I realized that "I" didn't even exist to start with, death became meaningless: "I" was free. We are all free. Joy resounds.

BH/Journal

IT GETS DARKER AND DARKER AND
THEN JESUS IS BORN.
Wendell Berry

WE ARE ALL JUST WALKING EACH OTHER HOME.
Baba Ram Dass

Dear Boys,

As you emerge from the cocoon of enforced schooling in your late teens, you may discover that many jobs will suck out your soul and reduce you to little more than a wage robot.

May I suggest that you tack the poet Walt Whitman's sermon to your bathroom mirror and refer to it frequently as you shave, which you may be up to even now. (Walt didn't seem to shave much)

This is what you shall do; Love the earth and sun and the animals, despise riches, give alms to everyone that asks, stand up for the stupid and crazy, devote your income and labor to others, hate tyrants, argue not concerning God, have patience and indulgence toward the people, take off your hat to nothing known or unknown or to any man or number of men . . . re-examine all you have been told at school or church or in any book, dismiss whatever insults your own soul, and your very flesh shall be a great poem and have the richest fluency not only in its words but in the silent lines of its lips and face and between the lashes of your eyes and in every motion and joint of your body.

Dear Boys,

As I finished assembling this collection and moved deeper into elderhood, I was suddenly laid out with serious heart problems. Outside my bedroom window a tiny wren took up residence and started a family in a bird house I had rescued from the dump and repaired. The wren—I guess he was a he—sang all day and would not shut up. Whenever I thought about packing it in, the wren's happy racket encouraged me to keep on. He preached defiant joy and new birth. His heart would not allow him to quit.

Blessings, courage to you for your pilgrim journey.

IT BEGAN IN MYSTERY AND IT WILL END IN MYSTERY, BUT WHAT A SAVAGE AND BEAUTIFUL COUNTRY LIES IN BETWEEN.

Diane Ackerman